Evaluation Activities
of Curriculum Projects

AMERICAN EDUCATIONAL RESEARCH ASSOCIATION
MONOGRAPH SERIES
ON
CURRICULUM EVALUATION

Committee on Curriculum Evaluation:
Harold Berlak
Leonard S. Cahen
Gary Hanna
Jack C. Merwin
James P. Shaver
Robert E. Stake
Louise L. Tyler

Coordinating Editor for this Volume:
Leonard S. Cahen

Editorial Consultants for this Volume:
J. Myron Atkin
Richard C. Cox
Robert E. Stake
Peter A. Taylor

American Educational Research Association
1126 Sixteenth Street, N.W.
Washington, D.C. 20036

Evaluation Activities of Curriculum Projects:

A Starting Point

Hulda Grobman

School of Education
New York University

Rand McNally & Company
Chicago

Rand McNally Education Series

B. Othanel Smith, Advisory Editor

All incidents and examples used in this monograph are true. Although several alternative citations could have been given, many of the positive examples are identified with a single curriculum project. No injustice to the accomplishments of other projects is intended. The author has not identified any negative examples in terms of where they occurred. Although the reader may know of such occurrences in a particular project, it is likely that the instances he is thinking of are not those the author had in mind, since most such problems have occurred in more than one project.

EVALUATION AND THE EVALUATOR

In the past decade we have seen educational innovation on a larger scale than ever before. Much of the innovation effort has been devoted to the area of curriculum development.

While evaluation has played a part in many of the Course Content Improvement Projects, we have a sketchy record, at best, of what the evaluation process was and what it contributed to the projects it was commissioned to serve.

The Committee directing the *AERA Monograph Series on Curriculum Evaluation* decided that at least one monograph should be devoted to a detailed report of the specific roles evaluation played during that hectic post-Sputnik decade in the innovation of curriculum materials. Dr. Hulda Grobman agreed to prepare a monograph on the topic of evaluation in the curriculum project. She brings a wide range of experience and background to her writings, based on her extensive experience as a consultant to many curriculum projects plus her long-term experience as evaluator of the Biological Sciences Curriculum Study (BSCS), a large-scale curriculum innovation activity designed to improve the teaching and learning of biology at the secondary school level.

Robert Stake (1967) pointed out in his introductory article to the first monograph of the AERA Monograph Series on Curriculum Evaluation that its ultimate purpose was to serve the practitioner. Dr. Grobman's contribution is directed primarily at this audience. The Monograph integrates positions, concepts, and real examples based on her involvement in and perceptions of many different curriculum innovation activities. It exposes the reader to the many facets of evaluation. The topics include the emerging and changing methods of the development of curriculum materials themselves, the distinctions and overlaps between the concepts of formative and summative evaluation, the issues underlying the decision to have the evaluation performed by outside agencies versus the decision to have the evaluation performed by members of the innovation staff, the controversy over the need to state objectives of programs in terms of observable behaviors, the need to explore and develop research paradigms for evaluation, the concept of the group versus the individual as the sampling unit in evaluation studies, the utilization of data (in its broadest sense) for purposes of feedback and modification of materials, and the very important subtle aspects of human interaction and rapport that must exist between the curriculum developer, the evaluator, and the consumer.

Hopefully, the Monograph will make the potential evaluator aware of the many aspects of evaluation and the multitude of talents and skills a contemporary evaluator should be able to bring to an evaluation problem. It has become obvious that new techniques and new ways of thinking must be brought to bear on the issues of evaluating educational systems, programs, and products. This is not a call to throw away all existing methodologies. Hopefully, future models of evaluation will continue to use techniques that are logically sound and have pay-off but will supplement and replace techniques and methods that are ineffective or fail to provide information for intelligent decision-making in the evaluation process.

It is an impossible task to prepare a document on evaluation for all educators. This volume is directed toward the educator who is inexperienced in formal evaluation. The consumer of curriculum research at the school district level will become aware of the wide range of activities included under the rubric of evaluation and, hopefully, will understand the need for school districts themselves to become involved in the evaluation process that must supplement the evaluation done by large-scale projects. The reader will find detailed discussions of topics ranging from the philosophical-theoretical-ethical to topics that might be described as administrative, the latter being based on the concept that adequate evaluation is determined in part by the quality and efficiency of the administrative framework in which the evaluation is undertaken. The reader will undoubtedly find that some of the topics in the Monograph are more relevant to his needs than others. Some topics will provide general information, while others, in more detailed form, will provide important starting points and directions for specific evaluation activities.

The Monograph reflects Dr. Grobman's involvement and experience with large-scale curriculum activities. The application of her points to small-scale evaluation projects and noncurriculum centered activities will require modification. However, the relevance of her advice will be apparent to evaluators who have helped with the smaller scale evaluation activities.

The author points out that the process of innovation has changed dramatically in the past ten years. We have likewise seen a parallel change in the methodology of evaluation. Many new concepts and ways of thinking about evaluation have emerged through the writings of Lee Cronbach, Michael Scriven, and Robert Stake, to mention only a few. We are in an era of emerging and changing thought about what evaluation is and how it best can be carried out. Strategies that were taken as axiomatic fifteen years ago are now frequently questioned. For example, the need for stating objectives in behavioral terms is one that few evaluators questioned before the post-Sputnik evaluation era. Today the topic is hotly debated.[1] Other emerging issues and topics include the study of the process of innovation, the logic of comparing outputs of competing curricula when the objectives and content of the curricula are logically inconsistent, the choice of the individual versus the group as the most generalizable sampling unit, the role of values in evaluation, and an understanding of the evaluation process as a part of applied behavioral science.

As educators we must now ask ourselves where we stand in our understanding of the evaluative process. Where are we going? What roles will evaluation be asked to play in future innovation activities? Do we know enough about evaluation to intelligently develop procedures for training the evaluators of the future?

The records and perceptions of curriculum evaluators should be preserved and studied so that we can take advantage of what was learned about the process of evaluation. The Grobman Monograph contributes to this record. Hopefully, additional contributions to the literature will come from other evaluators and innovators of the past decade, so that the full range of perceptions and observations can be made a part of the art, science, and historical perspectives of evaluation.

Leonard S. Cahen

BIBLIOGRAPHY

Atkin, J. Myron. Behavioral objectives in curriculum design. *Science Teacher.* 35, No. 5, May 1968, 27–30.

Ebel, Robert. Some comments on educational objectives. *School Review.* 75, No. 3, Autumn 1967, 261–66.

Eisner, E. W. Educational objectives: help or hinderance? *School Review.* 1967, 75, 250–66.

Hastings, J. Thomas. Educational objectives: some comments by J. Thomas Hastings. *Science Teacher.* 75, No. 3, Autumn 1967, 267–71.

Raths, James. Specificity as a threat to curriculum reform. Paper read at

---

[1]A symposium on the topic of behavioral objectives was presented at the 1968 meeting of the American Educational Research Association. The reader interested in this controversy should also refer to the papers of Eisner, Ebel, and Hastings for a discussion of the pros and cons of stating objectives in behavioral terms.

American Educational Research Association meeting, Chicago, February 1968.

Stake, Robert E. Toward a technology for the evaluation of educational programs. In *Perspectives of curriculum evaluation: AERA Monograph Series on Curriculum Evaluation.* No. *1*, 1–12. Chicago: Rand McNally, 1967.

Topham, W. James. Probing the validity of arguments against behavioral goals. Paper read at American Educational Research Association meeting, Chicago, February 1968.

CONTENTS

Startling and bizarre proposals may not do much harm as long as no one pays the slightest attention to them. It is a quite different matter when change becomes a fashion and when the plaudits of the crowd are the loudest for proposals that break most completely with tradition. The present social situation is already sufficiently unstable. There can be no profit in compounding this instability by making fundamental educational changes unless it can be clearly shown that the ultimate result will abundantly justify the intervening confusion.

William Bagley (1927)

The Context of Curriculum Evaluation

THE SCOPE OF EVALUATION

In the past, educational practice has generally followed what John Kenneth Galbraith (1958) calls "conventional wisdom," which associates truth with convenience and the good with the familiar and comfortable. Although conventional wisdom implies a lack of logical, rational thought in arriving at a course of action and might seem to imply a lack of evaluation, it does, in fact, involve a kind of evaluation—a nonsystematic, nonrational weighing of alternatives and the selection of the traditional rather than the divergent course of action.

For a long time, this has been the practice followed in evaluating curricula. Thus, much of our evaluation has consisted of unsystematic judgments of the goodness of something by authors, publishers, school superintendents or principals, teachers, parents, school boards, lay committees, and professors of education and of subject matter. The teacher who keeps using the same book each year and the principal who continues to operate his school on a forty-minute-per-subject schedule are evaluating in that they tacitly or deliberately continue to implement a traditional practice rather than change to a different one. They may or may not have data on which to base a decision. They may not even realize that continuing an existing practice is a decision. Yet these are decisions, and the process of making them is as evaluative as is the decision to change learning sequences after a systematic study of the effects of different sequencing in mathematics on computational achievement by sixth-grade children.

Today there is increasing concern with evaluation decisions and procedures, accompanied by a greater recognition that the decisions are evaluative in nature and should be based on the best evidence that can be made available. In this attempt to be systematic about evaluation, there is a tendency to equate evaluation with testing, and to assume that use of standardized tests guarantees an impartial, valid, adequate evaluation. To define evaluation in this way is to do an injustice to the curriculum, since all tests are not equally appropriate, and since tests can touch on only some of the aspects of evaluation.

Another interpretation of evaluation includes anything relevant to judging whether the curriculum is satisfactory in terms of implementing the aims of the persons creating, adopting, or adapting it, or of the society in which it exists. The evidence may be of many kinds. At times it will be the students' scores on tests. At other times it will be judgments by experts in history or mathematics, or in education or psychology. Or it may be the reactions of classroom visitors watching the materials in use. The rate of adoption by schools may serve as an evaluative criterion. Even the decision of the curriculum writers to keep working on the materials is evaluative, since it indicates that in their judgment the project has sufficient promise to be worthy of further effort. The financial supporters of a curriculum writing project are evaluating when they continue giving such support. Schools wishing to try out experimental materials are also evaluating, since this implies a decision that the materials are worthy of the time and effort of the school staff and students.

Here, curriculum evaluation will be considered from the standpoint of the curriculum project itself, and in the broadest context. It will be viewed as reflecting all systematic efforts of a project to assess the strengths and weaknesses of its activities and their usefulness.

WHAT IS THE CURRICULUM PROJECT

The last decade has seen the development of a new method of preparing classroom materials for students. Heretofore an individual author (or team of authors), sometimes entirely on his own initiative, at other times with encouragement or subsidy from a commercial publisher, wrote a book for the classroom; or, in some instances, the writing was done by someone on the publisher's regular staff. The manuscript was edited and published, and was either adopted and used till the next edition came out or was unsold and passed from the scene. Within a given subject area, there was generally little difference in subject matter coverage by the various texts available at a given time, because they were expected to fit into the existing school organization and teacher background and skills. Publishers could not afford to produce radically different materials, since innovative books would not sell. While there was frequent criticism of the inadequacies of existing curricula, only minimal change occurred, lending credence to the comment that, "It is harder to change the curriculum than it is to move a cemetery."[1]

More change has occurred in curriculum during the last ten years than in any previous decade in U.S. history, both in subject matter offered and in content within the subject field at the various grade levels. Doubtless, this reflects a wave of change throughout education, influencing many such hitherto sacred areas of pedagogy as size of class, number of teachers per class, assignment of students to grade levels, and assignment of students to rigid, year-long schedules. Insofar as subjects taught and the content of these subjects are concerned, many observers think that an even more important causal factor is the new method of preparing curriculum materials, coupled with new mechanisms for retooling teachers in their use.

During the past decade, a new process—using the curriculum project—has become an accepted medium for preparing classroom materials and for speeding up the innovative process in curriculum. A major stimulus to the curriculum project movement was the granting of substantial federal funds by the NSF,[2] for the preparation of materials to improve the teaching of high school science and mathematics. In 1956 the first such grant was given to PSSC, with grants to SMSG, CBA, BSCS, and CHEM Study following shortly.[3] By the mid-1960s, possibilities for use of NSF curriculum moneys were extended and other funds became available from the U.S. Office of Education as well as from private foundations, so that funding for curriculum projects now covers virtually all subject areas and grade levels. By 1967 there were over seventy such projects in science alone.

Curriculum projects have been sponsored through universities and colleges and, to a lesser extent, through such professional organizations as the Association of American Geographers and such nonprofit educational organizations as ESI (now EDC, Inc.). While the projects have varied in the processes used, there are many similarities in approach.[4] First, sources of dissatisfaction with existing curricula are

---

[1]Hurd (1962) documents seventy years of such criticism of science education, and the continuation, with little modification, of the very practices being criticized.

[2]A number of acronyms, such as PSSC and NSF will be used throughout this monograph. Appendix A provides the full title for each of these.

[3]UICSM, which predates PSSC, was organized in 1951 on a smaller scale and received its first outside grant in 1956 from the Carnegie Foundation.

[4]Unfortunately relatively little has been written about the process used by such groups in developing their materials. Wooton (1965), A. Grobman (in press), H. Grobman (forthcoming), and McCoy (in preparation) document three early curriculum projects, SMSG, BSCS, and UICSM. The newsletters published by many of the projects provide running descriptions of some of their activities and processes.

identified. Then, plans are made to prepare new materials. Teams of writers (usually including both school and college personnel) are brought together for a relatively short time to prepare experimental editions of new materials. These are tested in classroom situations. The materials are then revised and may again be tested, with another revision scheduled before release for general classroom use. A fairly typical project schedule might be:

1964	September	Start organizing project and making plans for change
1965	June-August	Hold summer writing conference to prepare new curriculum materials
	September	Start year-long trial use of preliminary experimental materials in 50 schools
1966	June-August	Hold second writing conference for revision of materials
	September	Start year-long trial use of revised experimental materials in 150 schools
1967	June-August	Prepare final edition of curriculum materials
	September	Continue limited school use of experimental edition pending availability of final edition
1968	September	Release final edition of course materials

This is an oversimplified calendar, but it does give some idea of the sequences in one major project task, the preparation of new materials.

Curriculum project work often carries far greater prestige than does that of an individual author or team of authors, a prestige that may smooth the way for radical innovation. The projects are not dependent for advance support upon a commercial publisher, since initially they are subsidized through noncommercial funding; thus, they can afford to be highly experimental. When their materials are ready for commercial distribution, the innovations have already met the test of experimental use in the classroom, and so the risk to the publisher is less and the difficulty in finding a suitable outlet is diminished. Some projects have funds for special preparation for teachers; for most subject areas, there is also the possibility of large-scale retraining of teachers through grants to colleges and universities and to school systems. Thus, a number of barriers to change are weakened or eliminated.

WHAT IS CURRICULUM

Since curriculum projects work on curriculum, a clear idea of the scope of this term is a prerequisite to an evaluation of their work. To the layman, curriculum is synonymous with the textbook, and much curriculum development and redevelopment in the past as well as at present has assumed that to change the book is to change the curriculum. The result of such a view has often been that the new curriculum is the same as the old, masquerading under a different name.

A number of recent curriculum projects have started with writing a book as the method for changing the curriculum (their funding may have limited them to this); such projects have found that changing the book has not resulted in the anticipated change in student learning. Teacher materials have been developed. Courses for retraining teachers in new subject matter have been instituted. Special equipment has been designed. Films for students (sometimes to replace the teacher who is not producing the desired outcomes), and films to train teachers have followed. Nonetheless, in some situations the classroom learning has not changed. Other factors may have been more influential in determining what is learned in the school, and these other factors may not have been favorable to the desired outcome. Thus, many of the curriculum developers have come to recognize some basis for the educational cliché that curriculum encompasses all school-oriented learning experiences of the child, including some unplanned ones that produce results diametrically opposed to the aims of the curriculum planners.

In curriculum evaluation it would be easier to concern oneself only with the textbook, or with the sum of instructional materials, including films, tapes, television programs, transparencies, supplemental readings, etc. However, the child does not learn only from these, and what he learns from these may be very clearly influenced by the other things that happen in the school. A curriculum assessment that concerns itself only with the instructional materials, without some understanding of the other variables in the situation, may conclude that certain results are produced, but may give no indication of why these are produced, or why different results ensue in different situations. Or it may conclude that the materials have failed, when the failure reflects a different factor.

As curriculum projects have broadened their views of what curriculum includes, the scope of many of their evaluative investigations has also expanded. From an initial concern with questions of whether the materials were intellectually sound and could be learned by students, many project evaluations have come to include questions about optimal sequencing, grade level placement, teaching styles, learning styles, and change process, and questions relevant to the adoption and use of materials in a wide variety of situations. This broader view is not a matter of empire building; rather it reflects an increased understanding of the complexity of the educative process and the change process. This does not mean that all curriculum projects now have or should have all-encompassing evaluation programs; what it does imply is that, beyond texts and the tests measuring cognitive achievement on these, there are many areas in curriculum evaluation that are reasonable and legitimate for inquiry in a project's curriculum evaluation.

Another change in the project's notion of the nature of curriculum has been in terms of the duration of the improvement effort. Initially the implication was that PSSC, SMSG, BSCS, CHEM Study, and CBA were temporary, short-term projects; this was the attitude of the NSF itself. Such projects would prepare new materials, the curriculum would then be satisfactory, and the projects could go out of business. But again, an educational cliché has proven valid: the projects learned through experience that curriculum revision is never finished. The present increasing rate of accumulation of knowledge is reflected in an increasingly rapid rate of obsolescence of textbooks. By the time a book is printed, it is already somewhat out of date; as the field it describes changes, so the course materials must change. In addition, as changes are made in course content and method in the lower grades, course materials prepared for the later grades should reflect this different preparation of students. Thus, change creates the need for more change.

The biologists have replaced the BSCS 1963 editions of their materials with 1968 revised editions. CHEM Study made provision for a revised edition within a few years of the commercial publication of its high school textbook. As such curriculum projects take a longer view of their jobs and reorganize their structure and operations to a more permanent basis, evaluation takes on a new look. The evaluation sponsored by a short-term, temporary organization is different from that which a longer-term activity can fund and needs. Thus, as the curriculum preparation activity is seen as a continuing one, the evaluative function changes in scope and duration.

THE POLITICS OF EVALUATION

A first, though often neglected, consideration in a curriculum project's evaluation is the extent to which systematic evaluation is politically feasible, that is, the extent to which the project can afford the consequences of evaluation. Systematic general evaluation is practical only when one can admit that the activities or materials being evaluated might not fully achieve the intended results. This is not to suggest that such a project is poorly run or has an incompetent staff; rather it involves a recognition of the implications of the word *experiment*.

An experiment can be either of two very different things. It can be a replication or demonstration of the known, or it can be an exploration of the unknown, the innovative and untried idea. The most productive experiments are explorations of the unknown. Not that educators should make irresponsible trials, but if their experiments are to be more than demonstrations of the known, success cannot be assured in advance. Despite this, some people believe that all responsible educational experiments should turn out exactly as anticipated. They reflect the attitude of the school principal who said, "Of course I encourage my teachers to experiment, provided they can guarantee it will work."

Unfortunately a few funding sources expect right answers every time; the NSF and OE have been notably realistic where some other funders have not. There are also some project policy boards that will not tolerate mistakes. In working with such groups, it does no good to cite the hundreds of unsuccessful trials it may take competent scientists to work out an effective polio vaccine or to design a more adequate jet engine. It is futile to point out that in science many breakthroughs have been reached through serendipity, through the accidental, chance occurrence that leads an astute observer to an answer to the problem under study or to another, equally important problem.

Within as well as outside the educational establishment, many see the lack of expected results in educational experiments as being incompetent and unforgivable. This was the situation faced by one curriculum project where the staff spent more time in trying to interpret test findings so that they would be acceptable, than it spent in planning the testing, in collecting and processing the data, and in using findings to improve materials and teaching. Obviously this project could not afford the kind of evaluation it had undertaken, and did not recognize this fact in advance.

In contrast to this no-mistakes-allowed situation, the BSCS, when planning its first experimental classroom materials, decided to prepare three parallel sets of biology course materials, with the hope that at least one would be satisfactory in the classroom. In effect, it was saying that although all three approaches made sense, all were highly experimental in terms of demands on tenth-grade teachers and students. Such a situation permits greater leeway for the curriculum builders and also gives greater freedom to the evaluator than would a situation where no failures can be tolerated.

It would be comfortable but unrealistic to condemn all sponsors who do not recognize the uncertain nature of innovative experiments. This does not solve the problem. Sponsors with limited vistas will continue to be part of the educational scene; it is difficult to turn down money, even when there are strings attached. For most projects it is generally not a matter of "Can we afford any gamble?" Rather, it is

"How much of a gamble can we afford?" The answer is different for each project, and as the project progresses, the threshold for tolerance of less than perfection can change. To some extent, the problem is one of education. Also, a project with a record of successes can better afford some temporary setbacks, some admission of limitations. Thus, as a project builds a reputation for quality and forthrightness, it is in a better position to admit some limitations. For example, after a decade of highly successful innovation in the mathematics curriculum, the UICSM director stated in a major address that his curriculum under-emphasized important computational skills. This was generally accepted as a serious but understandable gap in some excellent materials; such a statement during the first year or two of his project might have evoked a more negative reaction.

While it is never easy for project personnel to discuss the question of risks in evaluation, advance consideration is less difficult and healthier than later embarrassment, dilemma, and recrimination. Generally it will not occur to staff members to raise this point unless the evaluator prompts them to. Even after he does so, he may have to weigh the answers in terms of his own assessment of the situation. It is then up to him to decide whether the situation permits an evalua-tion approach that is intellectually honest, and to act accordingly. The researcher in a curriculum project is not in an ivy-covered tower, and he may be the first to face the dilemma resulting from an evaluation the group can ill afford.

THE ETHICS OF EVALUATION

Evaluative information is often obtained either without the subject's knowledge that the information is being obtained or without his knowledge of the use to which it will be put. At times such data gathering raises some serious ethical problems. Given a desire for measures that are not biased by the subject's awareness that he is being studied, some researchers have used "anonymous questionnaires" that are not really anonymous, that are later identified with the indi-viduals completing them. They may run interviews ostensibly for one purpose, when these have served a far different purpose. They have planted observers under another guise. Some researchers simply spy.

The justification for such activities is pragmatic: they are effective. They provide "clean" data, unbiased by the subject's awareness of be-ing observed or tested. Many such investigations would be considered an invasion of privacy by the investigator if he himself were the sub-ject spied upon; but unfortunately privacy may seem more precious when one's own privacy is involved.

The isolated incidents of parental objection to psychological testing and the overreacting by the school system involved perhaps have more justification than many researchers admit; in terms of basic rights to privacy, the protests may be too few rather than too many. The threat to individual privacy is not an empty one, as is indicated by the recent appointment of a Panel on Privacy and Behavioral Research by the President's Office of Science and Technology (*Science*, 1967). The case for scientific objectivity is relative, and there may be situations where the evaluator should consider whether the knowledge gained is jeopardizing his own integrity and that of the profession, and if so, whether it is worth this price.

PROJECT EVALUATION CONTRASTED WITH OTHER RESEARCH

In the past, curriculum research has rarely served as a basis for changing education. The prime consumers of educational research have been other researchers. Curriculum project evaluation does not fit this pattern. The major direction of evaluation research by the projects themselves is applied rather than basic. It is concerned with the here and now, with the practical and the immediate. Particularly during the period in which project materials are being developed, evaluation research serves as a basis for change. For example, the evaluator may be given a week to find out whether average eighth graders can understand a given reading passage, whether fourth graders can follow a particular set of instructions, or whether first grade teachers who are untrained in economics are better able to handle an economic concept presented in one way than in another. The evaluator's answers to such questions may be used immediately by project writers in their current materials preparation activities. Not all project evaluation is this immediate or simple, but much of it can have as direct an effect on the materials preparation.

In the same way that it is far easier for a critic to make armchair recommendations about American foreign policy than it is for the President to make foreign policy decisions, the researcher who is in the position of directly influencing educational practice is in a far different situation than the one who is engaged in a purely intellectual discussion of change. While not all evaluation activities or evaluators are taken seriously by their projects, they should be and often are. This puts the evaluator in a position of far-reaching responsibility, a situation many researchers have heretofore not given serious thought to.

For the most part the usual researcher in education pursues his one or two specialties; any branching out is usually in a closely allied field.

While the curriculum project evaluator may have the luxury of continuing to pursue an area of major interest, it is unlikely that his research activities will be limited to a single interest or even to closely allied interests. Thus, project evaluation requires more flexibility than much other educational research.

Compared with other educational research, there is less stability in project evaluation, in that the curriculum itself is emergent. As curriculum ideas work, they are pursued further; as they fail, they are modified or scrapped. In the same way, the evaluation is emergent; it must adapt to the rapidly changing experimental curriculum and to the other changing needs of the project. This does not mean that the evaluator operates on an *ad hoc* basis. He must plan; but there must be flexibility in such planning. (Unfortunately funding sources, failing to recognize this, may request such advance details as the statistical treatments to be used in two years' time, even though, long before that time has elapsed, the project may find that it no longer wants to collect the data originally anticipated.)

Perhaps *emergent* and *dynamic* are the two best adjectives to describe curriculum project evaluation. While these apply equally well to some other educational research, in most cases the project pace is faster. Curriculum evaluation is exciting, since the evaluator can see the results of his investigations reflected in educational practice. It is also dangerous, since there are few precedents and the evaluator is constantly on the firing line. If things go well with the project, it is the writers and the policy-makers who are responsible. If things go wrong, the responsibility may well fall on the evaluator.

Initially there was an expectation among many persons in educational research that evaluation by curriculum projects would follow the customary educational and psychological research practices. However, as the curriculum project movement has matured, there is also greater acceptance of the need for such new, often radically different procedures (Stake, 1967).[5]

There are a number of relevant factors that provide good reasons for not always following traditional procedures, or even procedures that may seem most efficient and effective in terms of getting research questions answered. In the evaluation activities of curriculum projects, some purists talk as though evaluation is the *raison d'être* of the project. For some, it may be. But for most, the development of curriculum, not the evaluation, is the basis for the project. Evaluation is a

---

[5]Stake (1968) includes a bibliography of recent thinking on evaluation in curriculum development as do items in the American Educational Research Monograph Series on curriculum evaluation (1967-_____). Also see Easley (1967).

service function; it is not the prime determinant of project focus and activity. Thus, the evaluation must fit into the project, not the project into the evaluation. Unless the evaluator is constantly aware of this distinction, his tenure with the project may be brief, and the evaluation information collected may not be used optimally.

Some conventional research procedures may interfere with the long-run acceptability of the project's materials, so that even if the curriculum is workable and excellent, the potential adopter may reject it because of an unfavorable image built during the evaluation. Some may interfere with other project activities or with other aspects of the evaluation itself. For example, the project will generally not be willing to postpone some curriculum building activities while waiting for additional statistical analyses, or to delay classroom tryouts of materials for one year, so that new tests to be used in the evaluation can be validated. If the evaluation disaffects the participating teachers— for example by giving them intelligence tests or asking for information on salary, a question many people resent—such teachers may not fully carry out their earlier commitments and so the evaluation may be jeopardized.

While some of the limitations on curriculum project research also affect other educational research, their impact on the former may be greater. On projects operating on a national basis, there is generally less direct teacher contact with the researcher, who, in much educational research is located in the area or at least in the same state or region as the teacher. And there is generally tremendous time pressure on the project and on the teacher working with the project. Participation in project research may require far more of a teacher than does his participation in other research experiments, since it is not simply a matter of letting an outsider observe or test in his classroom or of carrying out a minor experiment. The changes required of him both in subject coverage and in classroom process are more demanding. He also faces the problem of retooling for a different kind of approach, and this may involve throwing out years and years of accumulated equipment, lesson plans, and catalogues from suppliers, and starting over again. (This in itself is often a commendable improvement, but it does involve more work.)

Projects are also faced with testing imperfect, tentative products— the new, experimental classroom materials—often with untried evaluation instruments. Development of evaluation instruments may be concurrent with work on the experimental materials. Often there is not time for prior validation or even for rough tryout of tests in advance of their use in project evaluation; and for tests prepared to reflect learning specific to the new curriculum, the only appropriate tryout population is the experimental group itself, since it is the only group that has been exposed to the materials.

It has been suggested that as the curriculum project movement becomes more systematized, the time pressures on the evaluator will be reduced; as yet, there are no indications of such a letup. Today's projects are not so enthusiastic about evaluation that they are willing to give up a full year's work on materials in order to allow time for validating the instruments used in the evaluation. This may not be the situation in organizations that are primarily research oriented (for example, the Research and Development Centers), but today most curriculum projects are not so inclined.

2

What to Evaluate

Upon deciding to launch an evaluation, many a project director may indicate to his policy board and his evaluator that he wants a complete, optimal evaluation. Such a complete evaluation is not only impossible, it would probably also be undesirable. Evaluation is far more difficult and more expensive than many project directors realize, and a diffusion of the evaluation effort and money over too wide a spectrum of activities may result in failure to complete the job adequately.

There are far more evaluative questions than can be undertaken or than would pay off for a single curriculum. No single set of questions is suitable for all projects. Questions of concern to one project may be irrelevant or of minimal importance to another. Some curriculum developers have called in experts to provide a ready-made design for them. While suggestions from outsiders can be useful, having an outsider create the evaluation design has generally not worked very well, because questions important to the expert may not be important to the project. Some projects have reviewed the literature seeking an answer; others have visited similar projects. The experts, the literature search, and the visits may be relevant and useful, but they may not provide an instant, relevant design. If the evaluation is to be useful, each project must develop its own unique pattern, reflecting the interests and circumstances of the project and the clientele for whom the curriculum is patterned.

Optimally, planning for systematic evaluation should parallel project planning from the very beginning; however, it is never too late to do some systematic evaluation. The kind of evaluation and the nature of the evaluation design are influenced by: what is possible at that point in the project, when the evaluation information will be used, the purpose for which it will be used, who will use it, and the purposes of the project.

FORMATIVE AND SUMMATIVE EVALUATION

A unique feature of the curriculum project is the period for classroom tryout of experimental materials. Scriven (1967) calls this the period of *formative* evaluation; the period after the materials are completed, he terms the period of *summative* evaluation.[1] The entire purpose of the formative, tryout period is for feedback to the authors to improve the materials being developed. During the summative evaluation, assessment is of a finished product; here the purpose may be to compare the results with those of other projects, to describe to schools the uses of project materials, or to satisfy academic curiosity.

As Scriven himself recognizes, there is not a clear-cut distinction between these two phases; the formative evaluation does not stop before the summative evaluation can start. Much of the thinking relevant to formative evaluation remains germane as the project moves into the summative period, even though some new questions are added and some old ones are dropped or assume a different priority. Nonetheless, thinking about curriculum in terms of formative and summative periods is useful in determining appropriateness and timing of evaluation questions and activities and in determining whether the project itself and/or outsiders should be doing the evaluation.

If the project is to follow a schedule involving preparation of preliminary experimental editions prior to release of materials through general channels, then the most obvious first focus for evaluation is on information needed to make the end product better as a result of having been through this trial period. Once the materials are in final edition, the focus may shift to providing data to help school systems make decisions on adoption and use of materials; if the project will have a continuing concern with upgrading curricula, the focus may then shift to data needed for revising and supplementing its own materials as time goes on. The foci for the entire formative and summative evaluations need not be set definitively in the first weeks or even first years of a project. In fact, in some of the early projects, many participants might have been reluctant to embark on a long-term commitment had they realized what would ultimately be involved.

---

[1] In the time schedule on pages 6-7, the formative period lasts from September 1964 to September 1968; the summative period follows September 1968.

THE AUDIENCE FOR EVALUATION

One influence on the direction of evaluation is its potential audience. During the formative evaluation the project writers and policy makers are the prime, although not sole, audience for the evaluation efforts. During both formative and summative evaluations, the funders are generally concerned with progress. The schools participating in the experimental use of materials are interested and deserve reports of the efforts in which they are involved. For publicly funded projects, the public has a right to be kept informed on the use of its funds, and provisions for such information should be considered an obligation even where the funding agency does not require it. Beyond this, there is the potential user of the project materials, along with other educators and other projects for whom the information may be of interest and possible immediate value.

As one of its criteria of success, a curriculum project must consider whether it will eventually change what happens in the schools. Thus, its acceptability to the potential users is important. People and institutions are generally more amenable to change when they have time to get used to the idea. The evaluation program can be useful in the project's information program by providing information on the results to be expected with use of the materials and on the kinds of situations where these materials have been successful. The junior high school principal who starts to think about introducing a laboratory approach to science a year or two before he has to start allocating money for more lab equipment and supplies may be more receptive to the idea; he will also have more time for preparing the superintendent and board for the change. Fortunately the information needed for potential users can often be a by-product of the rest of the evaluation effort, or a modification of it.

INTERNAL VERSUS EXTERNAL EVALUATION

There has been some criticism of various curriculum projects because evaluations have been largely self-evaluations, with project staff evaluating the project's own work. Some argue that in order to guarantee a fair appraisal during the formative period, the project should hire an outsider to do the job, and that during the summative period, the evaluation should be entirely independent of the project. However, such procedures have serious limitations if the evaluation is to be optimally useful to the project.

In the formative period, if the purpose of the outside evaluator is to furnish an objective check on project work, his views on what is appropriate in the way of evaluation questions and ways of finding answers must prevail. On the other hand, if the project does not have the information it needs during the period of materials development, the formative evaluation is not optimally functional. For example, if the outsider considers one particular test a valid measure of the aims of the curriculum and the project considers it invalid, whose decision prevails? If it is the decision of the outsider, the project will not get the information it wants; if the decision of the project prevails, the outside evaluation no longer serves as an independent check.

Further, given the dynamic nature of project activities, it is difficult if not impossible for an outsider to keep abreast of the changing needs and emphases that should be reflected in the evaluation. Also, it is far easier for a staff evaluator to time the introduction of evaluation ideas and data as they are relevant, than it is for an outsider whose report may be received at the wrong moment, either when decisions have already been made or when people are too busy with other activities to give it the attention it merits.

Evaluation data are pertinent to many facets of project activities, and without an evaluator present on the staff, the relevance of evaluation data may go unnoticed at some key moments. For example, when project personnel are discussing future teacher training institutes, the evaluator can suggest personnel he has observed in the classroom who might serve on the training staff. He can comment on previous training activities in terms of whether the classroom activities he has seen reflect project goals. He can suggest areas that need more emphasis in teacher training or in the preparation of new materials. He can do on-the-spot reviews of new or revised materials as they are written to insure they take into account the feedback already received. As the project is planning a time schedule for the next year he can react in terms of what he has seen of schedules in the schools he has visited and in those from which he has questionnaire data. Thus, the evaluator can be a generally useful source of information and ideas about what is happening in the field, and through timing his comments appropriately—and spacing out his criticism judiciously, so that it does not become overwhelming—he may be more effective than is an outside evaluator's scheduled visit to the project or his lengthy, multipurpose evaluation report.

During the formative period, several of the early curriculum projects that initially turned over evaluation to outside agencies found it more satisfactory to direct the evaluation from within the project, while using outside consulting services. For others, where an outside evaluator visited the project on a periodic consulting basis, with no full-time staff member committed to evaluation between visits, the experience was frustrating to the evaluator and unproductive to the project. In fact, some of the organizations providing various evaluation services have been reluctant to work in situations where there is no evaluator on the project staff.

A few projects have discouraged all independent research during the formative period, since, if this is carried out in project experimental schools, it may bias the project evaluation, and if it is done in other schools, there is no guarantee that the researcher can provide full implementation of the curriculum, and so findings may be misleading. Furthermore, in independent research the time schedule often does not provide data in time to be useful to the project; data may not be available until the temporary, experimental edition of the curriculum has already been replaced, and so the findings are not relevant to an existing curriculum. At the same time, they may limit acceptability of the end product for reasons germane only to the earlier, out-of-print, experimental product.

During the summative period, there is a continuing project need for information on how and when the materials work and what the weaknesses and strengths are, in terms of the project's own concerns. This is important in facilitating later revision of the materials and in developing additional materials or programs to enhance their use. A further useful summative evaluation activity is the *longitudinal study* (a study of the same population over a period of time). Such a study can determine the extent to which learnings from a curriculum are retained and used in later years, a crucial test for any curriculum.

Much of the summative evaluation work can be done by outside investigators. Individual scholars and school systems should be investigating the usefulness of the materials in a variety of contexts, as well as replicating studies sponsored by the project. However, the project cannot afford to depend entirely on the timely completion of competent outside studies in precisely those areas in which it needs information. Furthermore, the project needs benchmarks for determining the appropriateness of outside investigations, since in many instances this cannot be determined from the data made available by other investigators. For example, one project, after widely quoting an external study from what is considered a reputable source, learned to its embarrassment that the data on which findings were based represented a nonrepresentative, two-stage sample of the experimental population (although the research report implied that the entire experimental population was used), and the statistical treatment was inappropriate for this sampling procedure.

Projects also need data for refuting findings of inappropriate studies. For example, the CEEB examinations in many fields have been slow to incorporate ideas from the new curricula or have produced omnibus tests, with some emphasis on the old curriculum and some on the new. After administering such tests, CEEB has issued statements to the effect that students in a traditional curriculum do as well as those in the new chemistry or the new biology, thereby implying that such students are equally well prepared for college. The curriculum projects counter this claim on theoretical grounds and with data that are not directly comparable, since the project data are not from parallel studies. In this controversy the position of the curriculum projects is not as strong or as convincing as it would be if they had comparative data from systematic studies of college-bound high school seniors or college freshmen. Thus, evaluation by the curriculum projects themselves would appear to be appropriate and useful, not only during the formative evaluation but also during the summative evaluation.

EVALUATION OF PRODUCT

Most curriculum projects are concerned with evaluating the curriculum materials or curriculum product. This evaluation can focus on the materials themselves, on whether the materials are valid in the sense of accuracy as well as in implementing the intent of the authors.[2] It can be what Easley (undated) calls "finding an optimal path through the discipline—a path that can be traveled by the largest number of students to appropriate ends. . . ." Thus, evaluation can look at the performance of the students using the materials, to ascertain whether new skills, attitudes, and behaviors have been attained. Such evaluation can be a *macro-evaluation* or a *micro-evaluation*. That is, one can ask a broad question, such as: Generally speaking, can students use the materials? Or one can look at a smaller segment or at a particular point in the materials and ask: Is a suitable teaching medium used here? Is the sequencing optimal? Are varied techniques needed for different teaching situations? (Anderson, forthcoming 1969, is an example of a micro-evaluation study.) Some projects will be interested in whether the student body as a whole changes, while others will be concerned with which individuals change and the nature and details of this change.

The curriculum study need not decide between the general and

---

[2]Gordon (1966) suggests some interesting ways of checking materials against the verbalized intents of their authors as well as in terms of the validity of the assumptions about pupils, instructional situations, and goal characteristics.

the more specific evaluation; probably it will be necessary to do at least some of each at the same time. However, perhaps for many projects the earlier macro-evaluation question of whether the general purposes are feasible will precede the later more detailed micro-evaluation look at segments of the materials to improve them. Emphasis on macro- or micro-evaluation will depend on the purpose of the particular project and on the participants and their interests. In either event, one must have an idea of the project's intent, that is, what its aims are and what hypotheses it is testing. The apparent simplicity of this statement is deceptive. There are several problems involved, including the exploratory nature of the job to be done, and the reluctance of the project personnel to take the time to state precise objectives.

SPECIFYING PROJECT AIMS

Those who favor precise statements of objectives in advance of work on materials and evaluation often cite the scientist as a relevant model. They say that the competent scientist decides precisely what he wants to do, systematically sets up a hypothesis, builds a logical design to test it, and then implements this design systematically and gets a yes or no answer. This is one of the myths of science. The good scientist may work this way, but he does not always do so, even though his final reports cite hypotheses and systematic experimental designs to test these. The great scientist may be the one who is freest to play around with ideas, to speculate on very tentative hypotheses, and to discard a hypothesis—even a systematically built one—when he comes across something far more interesting in his work and he is astute enough to recognize that the new possibility has more potential. Often his hypothesis comes after, rather than before, much of his research (Wilder, 1967). Today, with the project method of building curricula fairly young and with many projects still feeling their way, freedom to explore, before building detailed hypotheses or lists of objectives, is not necessarily license or lack of a scientific approach; it may be the most effective way of operating.

In the early days of the BSCS, the importance of preparing precisely stated objectives was repeatedly pointed out by one or two participants and the suggestion was repeatedly ignored by the remainder. While it is easy to criticize these biologists and biology educators, listing educational objectives is not the way they think about education, and if, at this point, the group had been forced to work on statements of objectives, undoubtedly many valuable contributors to the project would have pulled out. The existence of BSCS course materials, produced in record time, are evidence that it is possible to do a respectable job without an advance list of detailed objectives. Today, some years later, the BSCS does have some written objectives, but these are largely *emergent objectives*, developed as a concomitant to other work. Furthermore, the present list may be more realistic and imaginative than an advance list could have been. On the other hand, the AAAS Science Project, the first major project to focus on the specification of objectives in behavioral terms (Walbesser, 1963), was able to specify behavioral objectives in advance. Table 1 indicates the types of tasks or objectives that have been defined and the context in which these behaviors are to be demonstrated.

Reluctance to work on statements of objectives is not limited to scientists or science educators. For persons who have not done this work before, the problem is so difficult and so tied up in semantics that not only is this task in danger of bogging down, but the entire project may collapse. One project evaluator was convinced that unless behavioral objectives were clearly stated in advance in terms of observable and measurable behaviors of students or teachers, evaluation was impossible. He stated that unless his project prepared such a detailed list in advance of preparing classroom materials, he would leave the project. And the project did set up such objectives. However, faced with this ultimatum, some other projects would inquire just how soon the evaluator's departure might be expected.

Still, projects and their evaluators need some sense of direction. Sponsors know they want to improve the teaching of fifth-grade language skills or introduce anthropology into the grade school, and they are generally concerned with developing creative thinking and an inquiring mind. However, these mean different things to different people, and until the evaluator has some idea of what creative thinking or an inquiring mind means to the project, he can hardly plan an evaluation.

There are several things the evaluator can do to help the project clarify objectives. First, he can ask such questions as: "Is . . . what you mean?" "Is . . . the kind of child you would like to turn out?" "Do you want students to be able to do . . . ?" "Is . . . the kind of teaching you are talking about?" He can do some descriptive writing and some test writing and check these for reactions. It is far easier for the historian to look at a test question and say, "This is exactly what I am driving at," or, "That is not relevant," than it is for him to phrase a specific, detailed objective.

One group of elementary teachers working on an economics curriculum stated as an objective that fourth graders should "understand specialization of labor." To them, this was a clearly stated objective. These teachers, who had been writing objectives for years, were insulted at a suggestion that they receive training in writing objectives.

To reduce the ambiguity, the evaluator asked whether certain evaluation criteria—specific test questions and behaviors to be observed— were appropriate. By accepting some questions and techniques and rejecting others, the teachers began to focus on a more precise delineation of "understand specialization of labor." On some, they had clear notions of the expectations they held in common. For example, the evaluator asked, "After seeing a movie of an Eskimo culture, introduced with no reference to their classwork, would you expect any student to volunteer that the Eskimos were specializing, even though their activities differed from ours?" The teachers did not expect such behavior; they agreed that recognition of specialization was expected only in communities like theirs.[3] When confronted with other kinds of evaluative questions, the teachers were surprised to find either that they were not clear in their own minds about whether they expected a given type of response or that there was no consensus. The outcome of several hours of such questioning by the evaluator was a teacher request for time spent on clarifying objectives before talking about evaluation.

Another indirect way of developing objectives is through statements written for other purposes. For example, if no one on the project staff objects to a statement in a speech, article, or annual report describing the project, in effect this becomes a written objective of the project. This may not seem to be the most efficient way of specifying objectives, but it often works when nothing else seems to.

In defining objectives, two very different frameworks may be considered. First is that of Mager (1962), who states objectives in terms of observable and measurable immediate behavior. And second is that of Bloom (1956) and Krathwohl et al. (1964), who classify objectives in terms of the cognitive domain (knowledge and intellectual skills relevant to use of knowledge), the affective domain (attitudes and values), and the psychomotor domain (manipulative and motor skills), and within each of these domains develop a taxonomy or hierarchy of levels.[4] While these approaches are not deliberately juxtaposed by their authors, use of one may preclude extensive use of the other.[5]

With the Mager approach, for example, rather than state, "The

---

[3]The question here is not whether the teachers' expectations were appropriate, but rather that, prior to the question, they had not communicated them to the evaluator.

[4]The taxonomy of the psychomotor domain has not yet been developed.

[5]Mager (1962), Bloom (1956), and Krathwohl et al. (1964) are well worth reading, if the evaluator and project director are to be aware of the range of aims open to the project and of ways to verbalize these.

TABLE 1

SAMPLE OF BEHAVIORAL OBJECTIVES DEVELOPED BY THE AAAS COMMISSION ON SCIENCE EDUCATION, FOR SCIENCE–A PROCESS APPROACH, ITS ELEMENTARY SCHOOL SCIENCE CURRICULA.

Summary of the behavioral objectives and context for some of the exercises of a biological nature in Parts 1 to 5

Number of exercise in each Part and science process	What the child should be able to do at the end of the instruction of each exercise	Biological context of the exercise
	Part 1 (for Kindergarten)	
3-Obs	Identify an object and construct groups of objects on the basis of color, shape, texture, and size.	Assortment of apples, bananas, peaches, grapes, nuts.
4-Cl	Construct one-stage classifications of objects using characteristics selected by himself or someone else; state the criteria used for the classification.	Sets of leaves, nuts, and mono- and bivalve shells.
	Part 2 (for Grade One)	
2-S/T	Identify, name, and demonstrate symmetry of objects; state and demonstrate that some objects can be folded or cut in more than one way to produce matching halves.	Common edible fruits and vegetables.
8-Comm	Name properties of an object (color, length, shape, symmetry, texture, odor, and so on) so a second person can identify the object.	Pictures of animals.
	Part 3 (for Grade Two)	
12-Meas	Estimate linear dimensions of objects in centimeters, decimeters, or meters; observe an object of a known length or width and name a familiar object which is approximately the same length or width.	Children determine if a 20-meter long *Brontosaurus* or a 6-meter high *Tyrannosaurus* would fit in their classroom; lengths of children's pets are compared with objects in the classroom.
23-Pred	Demonstrate a method for collection and organization of data; construct a bar graph from the data; state a prediction based on the data in the graph; state how the prediction could be tested.	Survey of children's preferences (favorite animal, favorite flavor of ice cream); predictions about preferences of other children.

Part 4 (for Grade Three)

Code	Description	Materials
4-Inf	Distinguish between an observation and an inference; construct inferences from available evidence of relationships between animal tracks and characteristics of the environment in which the animal lives; demonstrate that inferences may be altered by additional observations.	Pictures of outlines of animal feet, bird beaks, and bird claws; broken nuts and acorns; logs of wood with animal borings; remains of animal homes (nests, cocoons); animal tracks in nature.
9-Obs	Identify stimuli in the environment of an animal; identify responses of an animal to a stimulus.	Responses of themselves, fish, and a turtle to various stimuli.

Part 5 (for Grade Four)

Code	Description	Materials
1-ID	Describe changes in the performance of an animal that indicate learning has taken place; construct a graph showing changes over a period of time.	Guinea pigs and a maze.
2-CV	Identify variables in an activity in which water moves within materials; identify variables which are manipulated or are held constant; state and demonstrate that water moves upward in some materials faster than in others; identify materials which have greater water-holding power than others.	Seeds imbibing water; soil; fabric.
12b-ID	Name a property to be measured as a means of describing variations in a population; demonstrate a procedure for measuring the property and for ordering groups of measurements; construct a graph of the frequency distribution of the measurements; state and apply a rule for finding the mode, median, mean, and range of a set of data, and identify each of these numbers on the graph.	Variation in pea pods and icicle radish plants.
14-DO	Identify, using a microscope, the small units of varying size and shape that make up living things; draw representations of these units; construct an operational definition of a cell in descriptive terms.	Cells of onion, lettuce, tomato, cucumber, celery, apple, and elodea.

Source: Edwin B. Kurtz, Jr. Biology in science—a process approach. *The American Biology Teacher*, March 1967, 29:3, 194. Reproduced with permission of the author and publisher.

student will understand how to use a library," one behavioral objective might be, "When given the full name of the author, the student can locate and record in his notebook the call numbers of all holdings in the school library, without assistance from librarians or other students." Or, "Using the card catalogue, the student will list in writing, in correct bibliographic form, three references suitable for use in preparing a term paper on Shakespeare's tragedies." Such statements communicate a clearer picture of expectations than do statements asking for "understanding," and, with the detailed statement, both student and teacher can readily determine whether the desired outcome has been achieved. Many of the tasks of education can be stated in such clear behavioral terms, thereby facilitating communication among project personnel and between the project and its audience of potential users, and giving direction to the evaluator.

In contrast with those who prefer behavioral statements of educational objectives, Bloom (1956) is concerned with classifying objectives in terms of level of cognitive skill, in an ascending hierarchy or taxonomy. The lowest and least complex in the hierarchy is the acquisition of knowledge; following are comprehension (translation, interpretation, extrapolation), application (use of abstractions in particular and concrete situations), analysis (analysis of elements of relationships and organizational principles), synthesis (organization of elements and parts to form a new whole), and evaluation (making of judgments about the value of material and methods for a given purpose).[6]

In the affective domain, there is also an ascending hierarchy or taxonomy, ranging from receiving or attending (simply listening and being willing to listen) to responding (which may be mere acquiescence or it may be willingness or even satisfaction in response), valuing (considering that a thing, phenomenon, or behavior has worth), organization of values into a rational system, and behavior characterized by a value or value complex (Krathwohl et al., 1964).

One difficulty in reconciling the behavioral objectives approach with a discussion of objectives in terms of the cognitive and affective hierarchies, is that the objectives most readily stated in behavioral terms deal with the lowest levels of the cognitive domain, with knowledge and comprehension (in the sense that these are used by Bloom), and with the first two levels of the affective domain, receiving and responding. However, most current curriculum projects have expressed primary concern with such higher cognitive levels as the ability to

---

[6]Appendix B contains a more detailed summary of the categories of the cognitive domain.

use knowledge in new situations, with developing creativity (which implies creation of a unique product, that is, synthesis and evaluation), and with other skills classified as analysis, synthesis, and evaluation.

Projects have also been concerned with the higher levels of the affective domain, with attitudes of students toward the subject and toward learning in general. They have deplored the lack of interest and enthusiasm of students who, in the past, have often been mere passive receivers of knowledge (attending level of the affective domain) or who have responded lethargically, or at times willingly but without the enthusiasm or desire to pursue the matter further, either in or out of school, and who have been personally unaffected by what they have learned in the classroom. There has been concern by the curriculum projects with building values that are operational (in the sense that students have internalized them and use them in everyday living) rather than with getting students to memorize lists of values that are given back on homework exercises or on exams. Thus, the aim of a history project is not to have the child give a memorized answer to the question, "Why is the study of history important?"; it is to develop a sensitivity for historical trends and for the idea of the continuity of events over time and the interaction of a myriad of forces at any given time producing new history in that time. It is concerned with the student reading history voluntarily and identifying familiar historical themes in out-of-school contexts; with a carry-over of ideas, skills, and values from the classroom into the student's general pattern of living and thinking.

To set behavioral objectives reflecting such concerns is extremely difficult and may not be possible; where it is possible, immediate observation of the behavior may be precluded. Measuring values is difficult, since many of our attitude measures are merely *self-reports*, that is, reports of what the respondent is willing and able to tell about himself. (Here the problem is not only the student's willingness to report honestly, but also the fact that he may not know what his operational values are; for example, many people have prejudices of which they are unaware.) Furthermore, what the student tells about himself may or may not be related to his behavior today or that of tomorrow.

Krathwohl (1967) classifies objectives as global (for example, citizenship), intermediate (course and unit objectives), and detailed (mastery and transfer of specific skills). He points out that the detailed objectives are the simplest to state behaviorally, though even here, it is impossible to specify all the situations in which the transfer may be demonstrated. However, Easley (undated) points out that in the curriculum building process used by UICSM, such detailed or specific objectives for individual lessons or portions of lessons would be impractical, since as ideas are tried out in the classroom, the writer-teacher must be "constantly alert for unexpected moves on the part of students which rule out the anticipated avenues of approach or which open up new avenues for continued exploration."

The following are further illustrations of the difficulty of stating objectives behaviorally and measuring achievement of desired behavior. Given the usual requirement in American schools that students study various facets of the social studies with emphasis on United States government and history, the number of college graduates who do not bother to vote, much less take an active part in politics, is witness to ineffective teaching for the last fifty years, if the purpose of these requirements is to build a commitment to democratic processes. To use adult voting records or political activity as measures of curricular effectiveness requires waiting until the student is of voting age and has the leisure to take part in politics. The student's participation in student government and what he says about the importance of voting or active candidacy while in school may be unrelated to his later performance.

Scientists are concerned with developing the kinds of students who will recognize and consider the biological ramifications of new problems arising twenty or thirty years hence. Today's test question on implications of air pollution is not necessarily more helpful in predicting students' behavior on the problems relevant to the year 2000 than was a question thirty years ago on the importance of cleanliness, in predicting present decision-making on problems of smog, water pollution, population control, or radioactive fallout, problems not in the curriculum in former years.

There is much current concern with the widespread feelings of hostility and alienation among youth. It seems likely that such hostility does not arise from a single stimulus. The results of stimuli aggravating hostility or alienation may not be evident for years, and, further, because of intervening factors, the influence of a single stimulus may never be identifiable. Thus, concern with reducing hostility would be difficult to include in a behavioral objective, yet it should certainly not be ignored as an educational aim for curriculum projects.

There is no consensus on the matter of statements of objectives. Obviously we need clearer statements than, "We want students to think," or "Students should understand the Constitution." Some insist that all objectives must be stated in immediately observable terms before materials are prepared and evaluated. Others, while approving the idea of behavioral objectives, oppose limiting objectives to those that are conceived in advance, can be stated behaviorally, and can be measured immediately (Atkin, 1963; Atkin, 1968; Tyler, 1966). To date, most projects have arrived at a middle ground, and even the projects most concerned with behavioral statements do not ignore evaluative evidence simply because it is not germane to their lists of specified behavioral objectives.

EVALUATION OF PROCESS

Product evaluation is only one part of the job. Without evaluation of the process of producing, trying out, and disseminating materials, the project may be defeating its own purpose, since the curriculum problem may be one of better implementation rather than one of more or different materials. Evaluation of process may include investigating the details of the project's operation in preparing materials, in trying them out, in packaging them, and in disseminating the finished product; it may focus on teacher training and teacher operation in the classroom; or it may look at how the program fits into other school programs, what kinds of schools adopt the program, and patterns of rejection of materials after adoption.

For projects continuing beyond a one-time writing effort—those going through revision processes on experimental editions or preparing several kinds of materials—evaluation of processes used during materials preparation can be extremely useful. Someone may complain that last year there were not enough stenographers, or that the writing staff was too large or too small, or that the deadlines were unrealistic; and changes are made the next time around. But such unsystematic review of process is not enough. People now talk glibly about "writing teams," "summer writing conferences," "year-long trial use in the schools," yet there is little beyond word-of-mouth descriptions to indicate just what a writing conference for any particular project involves, what kinds of decisions are made, and whether these are systematic decisions rather than something the project fell into. Simply a detailed descriptive study of the project's process would be useful. Studies of curriculum projects, parallel to the Smith (1966) and Hills (1966) studies of the dynamics of a research center, might make internal process of a curriculum project far more effective. And evaluation studies with as much descriptive information on evaluative treatment as that of Glaser et al. (1966) are important for the understanding of project work and for replication purposes.

Because of his very limited evaluation budget and the short-term nature of his project, the director of one small project rejected the idea of an evaluation of the process of materials development. He wanted simply an evaluation of the classroom use of the product. Yet a year later, when asked how things were going, he reported that there was little information on the trial use of materials, since virtually no one had attempted to use them. Even the teachers who had helped prepare the materials were not fully implementing them, and other teachers who had agreed to participate in the experimental use found them too cumbersome to bother with. The writers' failure to use their own materials probably reflected disaffection with the writing conference procedures, and the rejection by the other teachers apparently reflected the unwieldy packaging. Thus, though the project had been unwilling to spend time on process evaluation, in fact this was the only evaluation made during that year. Had the investigation of process started earlier, the subsequent difficulties might have been avoided.

Studies are needed on the relative advantages of various types of writing teams in preparing materials. Some projects have assumed that after one three-credit workshop in a subject area, a first-grade or tenth-grade teacher can prepare suitable materials for his grade level. Others have used college personnel to prepare first-grade materials, even when the writer has not been in a first-grade classroom since his own school days. Some projects seem to feel that high school materials should be prepared by subject specialists, while elementary materials —particularly those for the lower grades—need only a cursory review by a specialist after a classroom teacher has prepared a syllabus. Others have used varying proportions of school and college personnel on all writing teams. There has been little systematic study of whether any one of these formulas is more effective than another or of whether some are doomed to failure. This failure to examine process may reflect a feeling that such general procedural problems are someone else's job. However, some projects may continue to use ineffective methods, simply because they do not make it their business to find out what is effective.

Many projects have urged special teacher orientation in advance of use of the new materials. Some have urged that such preparation be given by the project itself rather than by outside institutions; others have urged preparation by subject specialists rather than educators, and some reverse this plea. These have been areas for heated argument, but for the most part the projects have not supported their arguments with data from systematic studies.

Even though many projects are concerned with the role teachers play in the classroom (for example, lecture versus discussion stimulator), the projects have done little to determine whether the teacher is playing the desired role and whether the special preparation for the new curriculum is a relevant factor. While there have been studies of the teacher's increased mastery of subject matter as a result of the special orientation for project materials, there has been less concern with the activities within the classroom which might show whether the teacher himself has changed and whether the pupils change. This was the case even where one project's data indicated that student performance on the project's tests was unrelated to the teacher's academic hours in the subject area. Studies of a large mathematics in-service institute (Pikaart and Hand, 1967), of NDEA history institutes (Thompson, 1966), and of NDEA Geography Institutes (Association of American Geographers, 1965) are worthy of emulation by projects.

If the goal of the curriculum innovator is to change the face of education, he must know not only whether his materials are academically, educationally, and psychologically respectable and that some students can learn them from some teachers, but also whether they will be acceptable and are being accepted in some or all school systems. Thus, the evaluation could well focus on the change process in relation to the curriculum, an area that has been badly neglected by projects. While there is considerable current research on change in relation to curriculum, this is too often independent of projects; and projects do not seem familiar with such research on change in schools as that of CASEA (Carlson, 1965; Carlson et al., 1965) and Brickell (1961), or with the research on change in anthropology, sociology, rural sociology, industry, and medicine (Rogers, 1962; Niehoff, 1966; Bennis, 1966). Much of this research is highly pertinent to the problems of introducing new materials and techniques into the schools, and provides ideas for process research by the curriculum projects.

Projects remain largely uninformed about what is happening to their materials after books are sold. When a visitor asked one principal the reason for the school's use of one rather than another of the new math programs, he replied that the school had ordered a traditional book and that the new math books were sent by mistake and came too late to return. Another principal mentioned to a project visitor that he was delighted to have the new biology for that year, since the parents expected the school to experiment each year and he was running short of experiments. In both instances, book adoption figures appear to indicate that these projects are implementing their goal, yet the classroom activities in such schools are probably incompatible with the projects' intents.

One of the few project-sponsored investigations of process is the JCEE investigation concerned with identifying characteristics in the environment compatible with development and implementation of new economics curriculum materials (JCEE, 1968). The focus is on why some implementation is more successful than others. Another project investigated the process of successfully introducing controversial subjects into the curriculum. This was an informal though systematic investigation of factors relevant to acceptance or rejection of new curricula incorporating sensitive subjects, and reflected the intense interest and personal activities of one project staff member, who probably would not even label his data-gathering activities as evaluative. Nonetheless, his testing of certain hypotheses about change in schools and school systems provided evaluative evidence that guided the project in further additions of controversial issues in later materials. Given the millions spent annually on materials development, certainly more projects should be asking such questions and making such observations.

While the earliest of the major curriculum projects that now have materials generally available—PSSC, BSCS, SMSG, CHEM Study, and CBA—are concerned about use of their materials, they have not made this part of their official evaluation programs. Yet they will not have fulfilled their mandate to improve education in their respective subject areas if they have made improvement possible but such improvement is not effected. The existence of better materials is only part of the job. Reporting that students in experimental classrooms perform in a noteworthy manner is not enough. Data on sales of materials are indicative of adoptions, but do not indicate reasons for the adoption, who tends to adopt the materials, whether the change in materials persists or is temporary, what appear to be the significant factors in such adoptions, and whether adoption of materials results in the intended changes in teaching and learning. Without such information, the evaluation is incomplete.

EVALUATION QUESTIONS AND PRIORITIES

Project evaluation activities would be far simpler if one could turn to a standard list of questions and use these in a given order, or even if one could turn to a master list and select from it. A number of questions have been mentioned thus far; Appendices C and D explore additional questions. While such lists may be useful, they do not provide all possible alternatives. Failure to include other possibilities may mean only that they have been overlooked. The problem is compounded by the fact that if the evaluation questions selected are not particularly appropriate to the desires and needs of the project, the project may find itself with expensive answers to questions it is not concerned with and lacking those answers it wants and needs.

In thinking about appropriate evaluation questions, it is certainly useful to review lists of possible questions, the evaluations of other projects,[7] and also the initial project aims. While such lists of aims may have serious omissions, they generally provide the major focus of the evaluation. Another way of checking to be sure that the project has considered the possibilities open to it is to think in terms of evaluation of product and of process, and within each of these, to look at the various steps in curriculum development and dissemination. For example, in product evaluation each experimental edition of each piece of curriculum material—book, pamphlet, test, film, teacher guide, laboratory checklist, etc.—can be considered individually, as well as in relation to the curriculum package or total product. The process evaluation can focus on preparation of materials, manner of dissemination, effectiveness of preparation for use of the materials (which includes not only teacher preparation but also the entire question of how school decisions to adopt materials are made and whether other needed adjustments in the system are made), and implementation in the classroom.

Another focus is on who will use the evaluation information—the project, the schools, educational researchers, the funding source—and what information each such audience will need. Evaluation questions may be thought of as short run and long run—what the project wants to know immediately or fairly soon and what, in the long run, must be known to judge project effectiveness. Unfortunately the projects as well as the funding sources have a proclivity for the here and now, rather than for the long run and often more significant evaluation investigations.

The criteria of suitability for any evaluation question are the interests of the project; these vary among projects, and, for any one project, they vary over the course of time. Unless the project is convinced of the usefulness of an evaluation focus, there is little likelihood of the evaluation being successfully completed and the findings being used. Early in the project the problem may be whether it is possible in introduce certain skills at the fourth grade or sixth grade. Later the concern may be in increasing the efficiency of introduction of these through adaptation of materials, changes in sequencing, addition of supplemental materials, modification of teaching techniques or teacher preparation; evaluation of long-term retention and performance; and the cumulative effect of a sequence of new materials. NLSMA, a five-year longitudinal study of mathematics skills of students in various

---

[7]Newsletters of other projects provide a useful though often neglected source of such information. Unfortunately these are not included in the various periodical indices and so the appropriate articles may be quite difficult to locate.

mathematics curricula, undertaken under SMSG auspices (Cahen, 1965), and smaller scale follow-up studies by UICSM and PSSC are noteworthy exceptions to the general lack of long-term evaluation efforts.

The setting of priorities in an evaluation program is not an empirical decision that can be made on an objective basis; priorities redect value judgments by the project staff based on a variety of factors. Further, if one project member has a research specialty or interest in a particular area—programming, self-concept of students, sequencing, adequacy of laboratory, teacher in-service preparation using micro-teaching (examination of an individual, short teaching act)—it will probably turn up in the evaluation; such freedom to pursue their interests is the price projects pay to obtain and retain first-rate academic staff members. On the other hand, such freedom may bring to the evaluation program not only a background of experience that makes all of the research more efficient, but also a much needed diversity among the evaluation programs of various projects.

Projects often find it worthwhile to pursue a question having fairly low priority when it is a by-product of other activities or when it may be obtained at minimal cost. In classroom tests, for example, the test answer sheets filled out by students usually contain the student's name and the school and teacher. For upper-elementary and secondary schools, additional questions concerning sex of student, sex of teacher, grade in school, and age of student can be added with no great increase in cost or student time. In fact, such items generally appear on standard answer sheets; yet they are often omitted from data cards, even though recording and processing such added data cost little and can give a better insight into the teaching-learning situation with that curriculum. Furthermore, such extra, low-cost information can be useful in helping interpret the findings on the major hypotheses and can also indicate some areas of possible error in statistical analyses. For example, one might assume that given a large sample of students in biology (a subject taken by most high school students), there would be the same number of boys and girls, that the boy-girl ratio would be constant for all groups or that the boy-girl ratio would not matter, since there is no reason why boys should have a particular advantage or disadvantage in learning biology. Yet, from by-product data, the BSCS learned that none of these assumptions was valid for its experimental groups. Thus, in making comparisons among groups, it was clearly important that the boy-girl ratio be considered, at least in terms of keeping the data separate during the data analysis stages.[8]

---

[8]*There is sufficient data in the literature documenting boy-girl differentials on a variety of achievement and attitude scales to warrant attention to this factor in all statistical treatments of classroom data.*

To date, one of the serious problems concerning project evaluation is the projects' narrow view of evaluation and of the usefulness of evaluation information. While some projects have done a better job than others, none has had an exemplary evaluation program. The vistas have been too narrow, and the evaluation activities too short term. Correcting this will be difficult. Merely telling project directors that evaluation information will be good for them will have little impact. Designing an evaluation the project is not enthusiastic about will not help much, since even if it is accepted, it probably will be ineffectively implemented and results will not be used optimally. To some extent, the project evaluator can educate the project's policy-makers about the usefulness of evaluative information. Certainly funding agencies could do more to stimulate more adequate and creative evaluation. But a major part of the burden for selling the value of adequate evaluation to projects rests with the educational researchers who are not on project staffs but who can be influential in communicating the importance of evaluation through their writings, speeches, and personal contacts. Unfortunately until fairly recently, much of this influence was negative. While project evaluations have had serious limitations, many research people have tended to focus exclusively on these rather than on the positive features. The projects with the most extensive evaluations seemed to receive the most criticism, since they had the most work available for criticism. Such criticism by research experts has soured a number of project policy-makers on evaluation. As one commented, "If the education experts keep telling us how completely rotten an evaluation job we are doing, why keep spending more money on it?" It is hardly a coincidence that the formal evaluation activities of his project have virtually ceased.

3

Whom to Evaluate—The Experimental Sample

In evaluation, concern with sampling is critical, since inadequacies of sampling will impose a limitation on the results. There is a current myth that if the sample is large enough, all biases will be randomized. Where random sampling techniques are not used (and such techniques are usually impractical for project evaluation), if there is a systematic bias in sampling techniques, increasing the size of sample will not automatically erase the bias. If one is not aware of the bias, he cannot compensate for it, as evidenced in the *Literary Digest* sampling fiasco of the 1930's.[1]

No single rule or criterion can be set for sample size or composition. It depends on what the investigator is looking for, the nature of his research design, and how much *sample attrition* (loss of sample during the research period) he may experience.

SAMPLE SIZE AND COMPOSITION

Undoubtedly larger samples are more expensive than smaller samples. However, if the sample is too small to permit the desired analyses at the end of the year, the ensuing waste can be even more expensive.

During the initial feasibility studies to determine whether experimental materials are at all practical under relatively optimal circumstances, perhaps only a few classes with relatively good teachers are needed. Such investigations, which often precede broader studies, may be nonstatistical, based primarily on observation and teacher reports,

---

[1] This was a completely inaccurate prediction of the outcome of the 1936 presidential election, based on a sample taken from telephone directory listings, during a period of the depression when a large, nonrandom sample of voters could not afford a home telephone. In this instance, increasing the size of the sample would not have lessened the overrepresentation of the relatively affluent voter. Had this bias been recognized in time, it still could not have been compensated for statistically, since voters without phones were entirely unrepresented.

or they may include some testing. For some projects, only half a dozen nearby classes are involved at this point; in others, because of antici- pated attrition, because the materials are not highly experimental, or because of other policy reasons, a somewhat larger sample is used.

A major consideration in selection of sample is the extent to which the project wants to generalize its findings for potential users. For the results of an evaluation of new literature materials, for example, Balti- more schools would be interested in whether cities similar to Baltimore have been able to use them successfully, not whether most American students or most urban students could use them. Emporia and Phoenix would be looking for still other prototypes. The literature project, too, may be concerned with the suitability of its curricula in each of these types of circumstances, rather than in more gross information on the "average" American student.

One project assumed that all schools are comparable, so data on any one school system could be compared directly with those of an- other and experience from one system would automatically be general- izable to others. This is not sound reasoning. The average level of ability of the student body varies from class to class within a school even when deliberate homogeneous grouping of students by ability is not used;[2] it varies widely among schools in the same district, and among districts and regions. This is important, since *general ability, as measured by standardized tests, is usually the most significant vari- able influencing student achievement scores, as well as scores on many attitude measures; often general ability is a more important variable than is use or nonuse of the project's experimental curriculum ma- terials.*[3]

As more precise information about strengths and limitations of the curriculum materials is desired, the sample should include prototypes of the various situations where materials will be used regularly, statis- tical descriptions of these situations, and sufficiently large subsamples of the different strata of this audience, so that one can examine these

---

[2]For example, in small high schools, where only one or two sections of physics are offered, the sections in English, mathematics, social studies, and foreign languages will probably be of lower ability during the periods when many bright students are taking physics. During periods in which Advanced Placement classes are meet- ing, sections in other subjects will be of lower ability.

[3]Some of the major differences among schools, such as cultural and socio-economic background of students, school dropout rate, and per cent of graduates going on to college, are reflected in measures of general ability.

While such measures do have cultural biases and therefore are not good indices for many purposes, they do provide those concerned with curricular offerings with a means of describing the student body, of checking composition of samples, and of adjusting data so that comparisons can be made.

individually where such examination—either statistical or nonstatistical —is desired. Sample size and composition must be modified if the project wants information on such questions as: Do the laboratory facilities or teacher background make a difference? Is one set of materials more appropriate than another in a given kind of school or teacher situation or for some students? Thus, size of sample reflects the degree of detail that is desired and the populations for which the project wants to generalize its findings.

The researcher is limited in the number of hours of testing time in any one classroom. Thus he may need more classes in order to have data on a greater number of testing instruments, with one group using one series of instruments and another group using a second series of instruments. Cronbach (1963) suggests a different strategy, which enables the researcher to obtain more information from the same number of classrooms without increasing the testing time. He suggests that different test items be used with different students in the class. Thus, in a class of thirty students, perhaps three or four different sets of items can be used. In this way, feedback to the project is multiplied, with no increase in testing time for students. One limitation of this system is that data are available only for groups, and not for individuals. Another is that teachers cannot use results of such testing for grading purposes, since not all students have the same questions and different sets of questions may be of differing difficulty levels. If this procedure is used for subject matter testing, either the project must prepare additional tests for grading, or teacher-made tests not completely appropriate to the curriculum aims may be used.

For its regular tenth-grade materials, the BSCS experimental samples reflected the decisions that the materials were intended for most tenth-grade students throughout the United States and that they were not for the poorest, most overcrowded schools, schools with no laboratory facilities, teachers without biology training, or the lowest ability students. Since the BSCS was concerned with the relative merits of each of its three sets of year-long course materials for rural, urban, and suburban schools and for schools in different geographical regions, the study population was drawn to give sufficient representation to different types of schools and localities. The sample attempted to exclude marginal school, laboratory, and teaching situations and teachers with no biology background. In contrast, the sample-selection criteria for studies by elementary school science projects would be far different, since the average elementary school teacher has little formal background in science and no access to laboratory facilities.

There is no point in evaluating use of curriculum materials in situations for which they are not intended, on the chance that they will work. In trying out its experimental materials, one project assumed that the schools themselves would be the best judge of the appropriateness of its materials and would not assign unsuitable materials to classes. This resulted in some highly sophisticated and lengthy junior high school social studies materials being assigned to eighth-grade students who were reading several years below grade level and were only marking time until reaching the legal age for leaving school. The only information garnered from this experiment, that the materials were patently unsuitable for such use and constituted a further irritant in an already difficult teaching situation, could have been obtained far more cheaply without a classroom test, by a thoughtful examination of the materials by a person experienced in teaching such groups. While it is not always possible to anticipate whether materials will be usable, particularly when these are quite different and more sophisticated than earlier curricula at the grade level, in cases such as this it makes better sense to try them out first on average students to determine ease of use, before inflicting them on lower ability students. (In the instance cited, the average students tested during the same year had difficulty understanding the materials.)

Where a study is specifically directed toward expanding the potential audience for the materials, if there is good reason to believe that hitherto untried uses of materials or techniques might be feasible or desirable, a small pilot tryout would appear to be indicated. Furthermore, if the experiment is not working out well, the project and school should be willing to stop it short of the scheduled completion date. In its experiments, the project should never forget that it is dealing with humans and that for the most part, it is using school systems that are publicly owned and supported.

While the experimental sample should reflect the potential users of the curriculum, a number of factors generally preclude obtaining a representative cross section. For example, there is the problem of teacher and student mobility. There are schools in America where only 5 per cent of the students in the school in September are still there in June. Such a school would be excellent for study of effect of pupil mobility on the curriculum and on learning, but it is not suitable for observing the effect of a year-long, radically new curriculum.

The project may want to look at the use of materials by interested teachers, disinterested teachers, or even hostile teachers. The sample may be biased when studies include only teachers who volunteer, since the volunteer may be the more interested, more alert teacher; however, many projects have learned that not all so-called volunteers are willing volunteers and that of the volunteers, not all are exemplary teachers.

Some critics feel that it is unfair for experimental teachers to be given advance or concurrent special preparation for the new curriculum. Such an argument ignores two points. First, teachers have already had specific training and experience in using conventional materials; thus, how does training for use of the new materials result in a bias? Second, giving the teachers a special training session is no more preju- dicial to the evaluation than is giving the students special new books, if both are part of an educational package planned by the project. The evaluation reports should specify that such special preparation is in- tegral to the new curriculum, should cite the fact that experimental teachers received this training, and should warn that other teachers not having it may not achieve the same results.

If the project plans extensive school visitation or periodic teacher meetings as part of its evaluation activities, experimental schools must be in geographic clusters, and these clusters must be located to permit visiting within the budget limitations of the project. Such considera- tions obviously limit the representative nature of the sample.

Given the various considerations in sampling, the project may choose a modified stratified sampling technique, with subsamples represented in a proportion different from that of their occurrence in the population. Some of this may be accidental, some deliberate. For example, if only a small proportion of the potential audience for the materials is in rural schools, proportionate representation of such schools in the total sample may not provide sufficient cases of rural students to permit examination of this potential audience. Given a larger representation of this group, such examination is possible, at the same time that any resulting bias in total sample data can be handled statistically.

Even if an accurate cross section of the population is possible in the planning stages of a particular investigation, this may not continue throughout the research. The sample may change between the time it is selected and the inauguration of the study. One cannot assume that the students of a particular teacher or school will be comparable from one year to the next. Schools may change ability grouping practices from one year to another; and through the years, school populations change, reflecting population mobility, greater school holding power, and new districting patterns for school attendance. Thus, when plans are made in the spring for the following year's study, schools or teachers designated in advance as fitting one subsample may no longer be in that category when school starts in the fall.

Some projects and some investigators have been interested in micro- evaluation, that is, in taking a detailed look at some single facet of the program, such as optimal sequencing, effect of educational media or enrichment, or how students go about solving a particular type of problem. In cases such as these, intensive data collection and rigorous control of variables are of more concern than is generalizability of findings. In some investigations more can be learned by an intensive look at five or ten children than from gross data on 1,000. Here, the considerations determining size of sample are far different. The investigator speculates on how few cases he can operate with and still answer the question he is asking. He may work with half a dozen children or with students of fifteen teachers, rather than with thousands of children and dozens of teachers. If this investigator is concerned with determining the generalizability of his findings, he can then replicate the study elsewhere in a number of small studies or can launch a single study with a larger sample.

Table 2 indicates size of samples for a number of different kinds of evaluation studies by the BSCS; some are feasibility studies, some micro-evaluation studies, and some macro-evaluation studies. While some of the small samples used by the BSCS were deliberately planned, the Second Course and Special Materials samples reflect budgetary limitations rather than a desire for this limited a sample.

EXPERIMENTAL DESIGN

The nature of the experimental design—how many groups or cells will be studied, whether there will be a control group, how many treatments there will be, and the sequencing of testing—is a major factor in determining size and nature of sample. A basic reference on the logic of experimental design is Campbell and Stanley (1963). However, one should not overlook the possibilities of designs developed in sociological and anthropological research (e.g., Riley, 1963; Lutz and Iannocone, in press), since many useful evaluative studies are basically sociological, socio-anthropological, or socio-psychological in nature. The choice of design depends on the questions the individual project wants answered, the resources of the project, and what, in the judgment of the project, is the best means of obtaining the answers.[4]

COOPERATIVE STUDIES

An unusual experimental design was created in the recent Cooperative Research Studies in First Grade Reading Instruction (Bond and Dykstra, 1967). Data were collected in twenty-seven individual research projects in reading instruction, after agreement was reached

---

[4]See also Stanley (Ed.) 1967.

TABLE 2

SIZE OF SAMPLE IN SELECTED BSCS EVALUATION STUDIES, AT THE START OF THE SCHOOL YEAR

BSCS Biology—regular classroom materials, including three parallel one-year courses for 10th grade average and above average students

Prelim. exper. edition, 1960–61	118 teachers, 14,000 stud.	10th grade, one-third of classes in each version. Only 105 teachers in Test Centers were included in the statistical analyses.
Revised exper. edition, 1961–62	541 teachers, 52,000 stud.	9th and 10th grade; three versions, and use and nonuse of supplementary materials. Only the 350 teachers in Test centers were included in the statistical evaluation. (Although testing was of 4 different supplemental materials, these were not distinguished in the statistical treatment.)
Commercial ed. 1964–65	100 teachers, 5,000* stud.	control group.
	ina** 11,000 stud.	to standardize parallel forms of tests for each of three versions 10th grade only. Included two special studies, on reading and on reading in science, with 1,000 students each.
1965–66	6 teachers, 128 stud.	Gallagher study of interaction.
	10 classes (prelim. study),	Anderson study of programming and sequencing. In preliminary study. 2 classes dropped during experiment.
	40 teachers, 1,000 stud.	

BSCS Special Materials—for low ability students

Prelim. exper. edition, 1963–64	37 teachers, 990 stud.	tryout of year-long special units as part of year-long BSCS or traditional course, primarily 10th grade.
Revised exper. edition, 1964–65	300 teachers, 9,000* stud.	tryout of year-long experimental materials, primarily 10th grade.
Commercial editions 1965–66	40 teachers, ina**	to standardize tests. Primarily 10th grade. 20 of these teachers and 426 students were included in the Combs-Gordon self-concept study, with 140 students given intensive study. (By the end of the year, of this special group, 316 of the total group and 111 of the intensive study subgroup were left.)

BSCS Biology Second Course—an advanced course to follow BSCS Biology

Feasibility study 1961–62	4 teachers,	60° stud.	Using 4 BSCS Laboratory Blocks as nucleus for course. (This was initiated by some BSCS teachers, rather than by the BSCS, and so was an unofficial experiment.)
Feasibility study 1962–63	22 teachers,	650° stud.	Using 3 BSCS Laboratory Blocks, with BSCS specially prepared supplemental materials to weave them together.
Experimental edition 1963–64	70 teachers,	2,000 stud.	10th, 11th, and 12th grades, depending on school program, some students from conventional first course, some from BSCS first course. Of teachers, 22 were selected and paid for by BSCS; (for training and books) others were covered by school systems. The statistical analysis included 1,117 complete cases from an initial group of 1,489 students on whom beginning of the year data were available; these students were from some 55 schools and probably represented some 60 teachers.

° Estimated
°° Information not available

Note: For many of its programs, the BSCS permitted only the teachers and pupils selected for the program to use materials during the preliminary tryout. For later experimental years, other teachers were permitted to use the materials, provided they had the requisite BSCS special preparation and their schools purchased books; such teachers also were asked to provide feedback, both through reports and testing.

Although the above data were taken from official BSCS reports, other BSCS reports may include slightly different figures, depending on whether they reflect anticipated participation or actual participation, whether they include all teachers in the program or only those whose test data are available throughout the year, etc. Some of the published figures are projections, some reflect attrition in sample, and some reflect the sample used for a special purpose (e.g. only cases of students where data are available on all tests given during the year).

Source: *BSCS Newsletters* Nos. 10, 12, 17, 19, 24, 30. Boulder, Colorado: BSCS, University of Colorado, P.O. Box 930.

among the projects on the minimum data to be collected and various procedures for the experiment. These included: duration of experiment, minimum sample size, nature of the sample, timing of testing, manner of administration of tests, and nature of instructions to teachers. Individual projects were not restricted to the agreed upon common measuring instruments or background data, and all data gathered could be analyzed by the project before being turned over to the Coordinating Center. (Since the layout of data processing cards was agreed upon in advance, each project merely sent duplicate cards to the Coordinating Center.)

Through the pooling of data, each project's findings not only remained as useful as they would have been in an individual project, but took on a far greater significance because of the comparisons with twenty-six other projects. In effect, each project had twenty-six other groups comparable to its experimental group, a situation no single project could have provided alone. Furthermore, the impact of the study has already been more significant than that of earlier individual reading studies, because—as is the case in many areas of education—findings in previous studies were often contradictory, perhaps because of the noncomparability of the experimental conditions in the various studies.[5]

Wider use of this cooperative technique holds tremendous potential for curriculum project research. It becomes more feasible as there are more projects in the same subject area and as projects in closely related fields attempt to achieve similar goals, using different subject matter as their vehicle. However, this type of joint venture requires careful control of significant variables, as well as agreement on common measurement instruments. Thus, it requires a high degree of cooperation and give-and-take among investigators in different institutions working under different auspices, a relationship that might be difficult to develop.

COMPARISON GROUPS

For any given situation, authorities do not agree on an optimal design. They do not even agree on the desirability of using *control* or comparison groups for curriculum project research. Cronbach (1963) argues against use of the control group; Scriven (1967) argues vigorously in favor of it. Many of the arguments concerning use of control

---

[5]For those interested in setting up similar cooperative research ventures, Bond and Dykstra (1967) and Stauffer (1967) will be useful.

groups are specific to the unusual position of the curriculum projects. For example, one cannot compare student learnings related to irrational numbers in mathematics or Keynesian theory in economics as taught with project materials with similar learnings from traditional materials, since the former were not taught in traditional curricula.

The *pre-entry status* of students (in terms of knowledge and skills relevant to the new curriculum before the students use this curriculum) can serve as a control for some purposes, but it makes little sense when the students obviously know nothing about the subject prior to use of the experimental materials. For example, at the beginning of the school year, giving ninth-grade students a sophisticated IME test using concepts related to energy may have several unfortunate consequences if they have never studied those concepts. First, the students may become frustrated and discouraged and may react as one student did when presented with a pre-entry test in another subject: "If this is what . . . is like, I want out." Furthermore, if pre-entry test scores are very low, statistical treatment may become difficult because of lower reliability of chance scores and problems of regression. If scores are at or below the *chance level* (for example, a score of fifteen or less on a sixty-item multiple-choice type test, with four possible answers for each item) statistical comparisons may not be meaningful. Similar psychological and statistical problems may arise in attempts to use tests developed for experimental curricula with control groups exposed to curricula that do not overlap the experimental curriculum.

Sometimes one large group of teachers or schools is identified as participating in the evaluation, and then random assignments are made to experimental and control groups. This practice may raise some school resentment; further, it does not take care of the problem of *contamination*, of spill-over of the experimental curriculum into the control classroom. While the difficulty is particularly severe when teachers in the same school are involved in control and experimental groups, it is not limited to this. In the BSCS 1962–63 evaluation, control group schools were selected only in localities in which no classroom sets of the experimental materials had been sold; yet, at the end of the year, when questionnaires to control group teachers asked whether any BSCS materials were being used in their classes, a number of control teachers replied, "Yes."

Where random assignment is not used, an attempt is generally made to match the control group to the experimental group selected by some other means. Here the question is: What is a proper control? Just as experimental groups cannot be selected randomly throughout the country, so control groups cannot be so selected. To attempt to match controls to experimental groups on other than a random basis requires a prediction of what variables will be important. This may be difficult in advance of the study. For example, in the BSCS 1961–62 evaluation, for the experimental population, variables significantly related to BSCS student achievement included student ability, sex of student, teacher salary, adequacy of laboratory, class size, and proportion of school's graduates going to college. Contrary to BSCS expectations the following were *not* significant variables: rural-urban-suburban composition of school population, size of school, length of class period, number of class periods per week, per pupil expenditure, and such teacher characteristics as age, years of experience, and number of undergraduate and graduate credits in biology. Furthermore, even after identification of six predictor variables, one-half of the variance of scores on the BSCS final exam remained unaccounted for. (Psychological Corporation, 1963). Even if we consider the unreliability of various measures, a considerable amount of the variance is still not accounted for.

To eliminate the problem of matching control and experimental groups, some researchers prefer having the same teacher provide two treatments: the experimental treatment to some classes and the control treatment to others. Even though the teacher may not use the same materials with both classes, some difficulties may still arise. If it is the method of implementing materials rather than the materials alone that are the key to the curriculum, is there really an experimental and a control situation? Can a teacher use an inquiry approach effectively from 9:00-11:00 a.m. each day and a dogmatic approach from 12:00-2:00 p.m.? If, in testing supplemental materials such as a series of films, a teacher is asked to use the film with some classes only, the teacher knows that the control classes are missing an enrichment experience and so will need another type of enrichment. Also, the time not devoted to the film must be taken up with another activity. Thus, the control is no longer the intended control, since the classroom situation for the control is not what it would have been had no experiment been undertaken.

SAMPLE ATTRITION

Despite initial care in selecting participating schools and teachers, loss of cases in the original sample is bound to occur and may run as high as one-quarter or more of the total cases. Furthermore, this attrition does not necessarily occur evenly throughout the sample. For example, in the BSCS 1961–62 evaluation, although an initial sample of ninth graders was divided evenly among three different treatments—

one-third used Blue Version, one-third Green Version, and one-third Yellow Version—for the end-of-year analysis there were half as many students remaining in Blue as in either Yellow or Green Versions (Wallace, 1963). Such attrition raises two possible problems: that the analysis groups may become too small for analysis and that bias may exist because of over- or underrepresentation of some segments of the experimental population. Thus, the initial sample should be large enough to accommodate some sample losses, and care must be taken to ensure that the sample in the statistical analyses has the desired balance or that this is compensated for statistically.

Sample attrition can result from a variety of causes. Natural events can take a heavy toll. One project lost a considerable number of teachers when a hurricane prevented some two dozen teachers from attending the requisite advance teacher briefing and there was neither time nor budget to schedule an additional one. In another area flooding of the book warehouse ruined the books for several thousand experimental students; by the time these books could be replaced, one month of the school year had been lost.

Teachers may move from one school to another at the last minute, or their teaching assignments may be changed. Teachers get sick; they have babies; they break limbs; they have coronaries; they are drafted or mobilized in Reserve or National Guard units. When Martin Company of Denver or Boeing in San Diego loses a major defense contract, the student body in local schools can change radically overnight as parents move elsewhere to find work; a new large contract can also disrupt the experimental sample by flooding classes with new students as workers move into an area.

Automatic mid-year reassignments of students to class sections can constitute a serious threat to sample stability in junior and senior high schools. This was the practice in a school system where one class section in each of six schools was participating in a year-long sequential curriculum experiment. During the second semester of the course, each experimental class had only five or six students remaining from the original thirty-five students starting that curriculum in September. Data on even these few were worthless, since the second semester of these classes was not representative of learning experiences in classes where continuity from one semester to another was possible.

Every school has some student turnover during the year. Turnover not only varies from one school to another, but it also varies by grade level and subject. For example, ninth and tenth grades are high dropout years, as students reach the age level for leaving school; college preparatory courses may have fewer dropouts than general courses. The senior class in high school is often more stable than other classes, possibly because parents hesitate to move their children during their last year in high school, and most of those students dropping out before graduation have already left.

Based on the assumption that students in school at the start of the year continue throughout the year, one project compared mean achievement scores for classes at the start of the year with mean achievement scores at the end of the year; the project failed to realize that this comparison did *not* provide information on student gains through the school year, since the before-course and after-course groups were not identical. To measure change through the year, comparisons must be of the same students, not of one group of students at the start of the year and of a somewhat different group of students at the end, with no information on the similarity of the pre-test and post-test groups. Even if one is concerned only with the end-of-course achievement, if the evaluation is of a particular course sequence, one should be sure that the students included in end-of-year data were exposed to the entire sequence; otherwise findings may be biased by scores of some students who have been in the course only weeks or months.

To eliminate this problem, many studies use a beginning-of-year test score (such as a score on a general ability test administered in September or October) as a benchmark for inclusion of cases in the end-of-year study. These ability scores provide a roster against which the later test returns can be checked. Year-end analyses are then limited to those cases in which the student was in the experiment at all testing points throughout the sequence. The same rosters can provide a rough idea of class turnover and so reflect the extent to which a normal class teaching situation is maintained.

Particularly when the project evaluation covers a large geographical area and direct contact with schools is not on a day-to-day basis, it is difficult to determine in advance the extent to which participating schools and teachers will meet the criteria required by the research design. For example, one may get commitments in advance that at least 80 per cent of the pupils will be at a particular grade level or ability range; or that teachers will have had a certain special preparation for the work; or that the participating teacher will have a minimum of 100 students at the grade level. But this may not materialize.

Many teachers will see that all tests are administered as scheduled and that answer sheets are returned to the project. Some, however, will not. If end-of-year tests are not given, or if they are given but answer sheets are not returned to the project before school closes in the spring, they are beyond retrieving. Further loss in sample can result from teachers who are conscientious about giving tests and returning answer sheets but who fail to use the experimental materials in the manner required by the research design. Often such lapses cannot be anticipated and by the time they are discovered, it is too late to take remedial action. Such situations mean the loss of all students of the teachers involved, a more serious loss than is experienced when a few students miss an exam or move away.

With micro-evaluation, there is usually closer contact with the experimental schools and there is less problem of the schools' overlooking commitments or of changes in commitments being made without the investigator's knowledge. But even here, there may be some attrition. However, for such short-term projects as measurement of one or two learning sequences, this is far less of a problem than for longer experiments.

How to Evaluate

SOME GENERAL CONSIDERATIONS AND PROBLEMS IN DATA COLLECTION AND INTERPRETATION

For many years educators have smarted under the indictment that they are not scientific. There is currently an assumption that if one wants to be scientific, one must have quantifiable data; and the more complex the data and the computer manipulations, the more scientific one becomes. There is also an aura of infallibility about statistical findings. Yet the attempt to rely too heavily on statistics and computers may give a less valid rather than a more valid result. This is not to imply that testing is bad, that tests cannot give useful and unique information, or that one should not use computers. Rather, it is to caution against blind faith in reports based on test data, and a strong plea for the use of a variety of evaluation techniques to validate test results and facilitate their interpretation. Given this variety of sources of evaluative feedback, information should be treated cumulatively rather than be compartmentalized. Contradictions and ambiguities should be investigated thoroughly.

Often sophisticated statistical procedures lend credence to highly tentative, preliminary, and imperfect data. Evaluation findings must be considered in the context of tests that are themselves tentative, of curriculum materials that are unpolished, and of teachers who are completely new to the manner of presentation and possibly even to the subject itself. Thus, student scores on such tests can have real but still limited value for interpretative purposes.

There is also a tendency to overlook the possibility that wrong data may have been put into the computer, that the computer may have been inadequately programmed or may have made an electronic error or a magnetic recording error, or that some major variables no one has been aware of may have biased the data. These are not idle fears. There are currently hundreds of studies of student progress under way where punching of data cards is not verified, or where the teacher reports of test scores are accepted as accurate, even though teacher scoring of objective tests may be highly inaccurate. (Often it is not even mentioned in the reports that the data are based on such manual scoring by teachers.) Further, very limited instructions on how to administer the test may result in noncomparable data from different teachers.

The interpreter of data generally assumes that standard or requested procedures have been followed. Yet human error is just as possible and as serious as inadequate programming or machine inadequacies and may be even more difficult to identify. The following examples of such problems are particularly disturbing, since they would be difficult to anticipate and prevent. One project, using student scores on the project's own test, compared classes of those teachers who observers agreed were implementing the spirit of the new curriculum properly with classes of the remainder of the experimental group. Based on machine tabulations done by an outside agency, the results indicated that students of the better teachers did *less* well than the remainder of the experimental students. With further probing, it was discovered that through an oversight by a clerical employee of the agency a non-random sampling of students pulled for an earlier study had not been returned to the data pool, thus leaving a depleted, completely non-representative group of students for this new study. An outsider's first reaction to this near catastrophe might be, "But this couldn't happen to us." That was what this project thought, too.

After two years' work with one computer center, another curriculum project learned that the transfer of data to data cards had never been verified. The project identified this problem when its evaluator scanned IBM tabulation sheets in which 2 per cent of the scores were impossible; that is, scores were recorded for nonexistent response options. Perhaps a 2 per cent error in this case was not serious, but even if one could make such a questionable assumption, one might well wonder how many answers had been incorrectly punched into the possible codes and so could not be identified through such scanning. No one in the curriculum project had ever thought to ask about verification of punching, since it was assumed that this was a standard procedure of computer services. Yet, today some computer work for curriculum studies at the more prestigious universities in America does not include such verification.

One project was given assurance by experimental schools that all participating students were at the ninth-grade level. It was fortunate that a student grade designation was entered on data cards and was routinely tabulated, since it was through this means that the project learned that some entire classes were at the eighth-grade level, some included seventh, eighth, and ninth graders in a single class, and, in one school, all participating students were eleventh graders. Had there been no grade level information included in the analysis, interpretation of results would have been distorted.

The interpreter of statistical data may forget that there is always a statistical chance that despite his impeccable sampling methods, the sample he has chosen may not be representative of the total population from which it is drawn. This may be one chance in 1,000 or one in 1,000,000, but in systematic sampling this can and sometimes does occur. In the statistical work for one project, each of two successive 1,000-case samples of the test population was significantly different from the total population. Given adequate sampling techniques, the chance of this occurring twice was almost impossible, yet it did occur.

Even accurate statistical evidence can be highly misleading. For example, the increase in participation in science fairs can mean not greater interest in science but rather a new requirement that all students must participate or that participation is a prerequisite to a grade of B or A. An increased number of science fair winners may not be relevant; it may only reflect increased pressure on students, which results in more parents doing science fair projects for their children. An increase in the number of students making high scores on any test, whether it is a scholarship test, a prize test, or an Advanced Placement test, should be considered as positive evidence only after an examination of the contents of the test. That students from one curriculum do better on a given test is noteworthy only if the test measures something the curriculum is concerned with. This is not necessarily the case, even with prestige tests.

Some consider evidence of later success in college a criterion of success for a curriculum. Unfortunately some of the most imaginative curricula do not prepare students for college; here, the fault may lie with the college curriculum rather than with the high school curriculum. If students are taught to inquire, to be creative and self-directing in high school, they may not be as well prepared for a traditional college approach as are students from a traditional, lock-step high school program.

It is important that the evaluator gather background information to permit adequate interpretation of the statistical data, since the apparent failure of curriculum materials in the classroom may have nothing to do with the materials themselves. It may result from something as simple as use of chemicals which have lost strength, the late arrival of supplemental materials, the breakdown of a film projector so that some basic audio-visual materials were not used, or the scheduling of a series of pep rallies so that some part of an important daily sequence was omitted. It may be the result of a severe flu epidemic causing considerable loss of teaching time. Or it may result from the failure of a teacher to carry out an experiment in the proper sequence or to use the appropriate teaching approach. The identification of these factors is an integral part of the evaluation.

In one kindergarten reading-readiness experiment, a basic hypothesis was concerned with the sequence of presentation of sound. A project evaluator visiting classrooms in mid-November was disturbed that the class was behind schedule. The teacher assured him that it was perfectly all right, since one of the later units had already been covered. Earlier that month, for "show-and-tell," one child had brought in a turtle, and, even though the *tu* sound (as in *turtle*) was not scheduled until much later in the experiment, "this seemed to be too good an opportunity to miss." For years, this teacher had been told to capitalize on students' interests; she was doing just that, with no thought that she was jeopardizing the experiment.

In a junior high social studies unit, intended primarily to promote an understanding of parallels in history, one teacher had students go through the book in class, reading sentences aloud and explaining their meaning in the precise historical context being discussed. No suggestions for current relevance were ever made, and any openings for such discussions and for drawing parallels among several different historical periods were patently ignored. For such students, any test for broader relevance would indicate the ineffectiveness of the materials; yet the problem may be not the materials but rather the mundane, narrow presentation. And what this teacher tells the project about his presentation may not reflect what actually took place in the classroom.

If a teacher reports that a given laboratory experiment is unworkable, it is pertinent to consider whether the teacher has a sufficient grasp of the subject to guide students through this particular experiment; the teacher's report may mean that the experiment is usable only by teachers who have a particularly good grasp of the subject area. Or the school's laboratory equipment may be minimal. For many experiments, it is imperative to have running water, electric and gas outlets; if these are not available, the evaluation feedback from the school takes on a different meaning. Or a given teacher may be completely hostile to the new materials, and, given this attitude, nothing could possibly work well. Or he may be insecure with anything new and may need time to feel comfortable with new techniques and materials. These limitations do not mean that such teacher feedback is worthless, but rather that it should be considered in the context in which it is developed.

For curriculum evaluation purposes, there would appear to be no single evaluative technique or instrument that can safely be used to the exclusion of other kinds of feedback. Equally important, if the results from each technique are not consistent with information obtained from other techniques, and there is no apparent, reasonable explanation for the inconsistency, further probing is essential.

The desirability of using a multiplicity of approaches to educational research is well stated in Webb, Campbell, Schwartz, and Sechrest (1966:174–5).

> If no single measurement class is perfect, neither is any scientifically useless. . . .
> This does not trouble us, nor does it argue against their use, for the most fertile search for validity comes from a combined series of different measures, each with its idiosyncratic weaknesses, each pointed to a single hypothesis. When a hypothesis can survive the confrontation of a series of complementary methods of testing, it contains a degree of validity unattainable by one tested within the more constricted framework of a single method. . . .
> . . . the notion of a single "critical experiment" is erroneous. *There must be a series of linked critical experiments each testing a different outcropping of the hypothesis.* It is through triangulation of data procured from different measurement classes that the investigator can most effectively strip of plausibility rival explanations for his comparison. The usual procedural question asked is, Which of the several available data-collection methods will be best for my research problem? We suggest the alternative question: Which set of methods will be best?—with "best" defined as a series which provides data to test the most significant threats to a comparison with a reasonable expenditure of resources.

SOME EVALUATION TECHNIQUES AND STRATEGIES

Tests are valuable evaluative tools, but they are only one of many sources of evaluative evidence. No test can determine whether the course content is accurate or up to date; it cannot indicate why something has gone wrong but only provide evidence that it did go wrong. At present some aspects of evaluation cannot be quantified. For some materials, evaluation is possible only in terms of short-term, relatively narrow objectives. (A five-minute movie can be evaluated in terms of knowledge gained or of student enjoyment. It can hardly be expected to make a difference in semester scores on a test of broad objectives.)

Thus, the evaluation strategies chosen for a given purpose should reflect a consideration of the variety of approaches possible and their appropriateness for this particular situation. The following summary does not attempt to include all the alternatives, and new ones are constantly being introduced and old ones modified. The most frequently used approaches can be categorized as reviews, school visits, teacher feedback, questionnaires, and tests.

REVIEWS OF MATERIALS

During the formative evaluation stage, reviews by experts, professionals in the subject area, psychologists, and educators are useful, even when the writers themselves are specialists in these fields. Experts in related disciplines can be useful; for example, the CHEM Study director reviewed BSCS materials in terms of the chemistry included as well as in terms of how the biology materials fit in with the CHEM Study course that follows biology for many students.

The matter of obtaining the desired coverage by reviewers is not simple. While apparently everyone reserves the right to criticize, not everyone is willing to give the time required for a systematic review of materials. Further, psychologists asked to review biology materials from the standpoint of learning theory may confine their comments to the physiology of the senses or to a criticism of relative emphases on different areas of science, basing their views on the science they remember from undergraduate days; educators who last took a history course twenty years ago may review as historians; and historians may focus on what they think sixth graders are capable of doing, when the only sixth grader they have talked to in decades is a grandchild. Despite clearly stated deadlines, reviews may not arrive until it is too late to incorporate the ideas into revised materials, though failure to incorporate these ideas may antagonize the very reviewer who ignored the deadline.

Furthermore, the expert's testimony must be considered in context. If he objects to the short shrift given conventional formulas in chemistry, or feels that oceanography deserves more pages in the earth science treatment, or disapproves of the omission of some of his favorite dates and heroes from the history materials or of Sir Walter Scott and George Eliot from the required reading in English literature, this may represent a personal bias rather than a broad view of the current field, the most promising trends, and the basic purposes of the project. Even when such reviews are not relevant, they may embarrass the project by turning up publicly at a later date.

Despite such difficulties, during the formative evaluation the review process can add to the integrity and usefulness of the materials. Also many of the reviewers would never have read these materials without the review assignment, and this reading can build a respect for the project and its work among highly influential professional groups.

VISITS

No project can afford to omit classroom visits, and such visits can serve a variety of purposes. Visits can serve to verify other feedback or to put it in a more meaningful context. Teachers who are reluctant to write criticism or who find writing difficult may talk quite openly in a face-to-face encounter. Conversation with school officials, teachers, students, and parents can elicit information that cannot be provided by questionnaires and may open up new avenues of thought not previously considered by the project.

Visits by Writers

Many project writers have little familiarity with the grade level for which they are writing or with the teachers who teach this subject matter. Here, classroom visits can improve the writers' perspective and also can make the written feedback more acceptable. Thus, the college anthropology professor, working with a junior high school curriculum project, may gain a greater respect for the teacher, the students, and the rest of the curriculum by spending a few hours trying out his materials in classrooms. This does not make him an expert on curriculum or on the junior high school or even on whether the materials are working, but it can give him a sense of reality difficult if not impossible to obtain without a visit. In a number of projects, writers have been so intrigued by the classroom visits that they have returned again and again, and some have taught units of the materials they have prepared.

Unstructured Visits by Other Staff Members

The project staff member has a different function in his visits—that of gathering direct feedback to evaluate, summarize, and pass on to others. If he is to pick up all the clues that are available to him, this visitor should be a sensitive observer with some background in what schools are like. He should also be completely conversant with the materials and with the project's aims.

Some projects find a visitor checklist useful for recording specific information (length of period, size of class, and adequacy of classroom for number of students and the type of activity required by the curriculum), some of which may merely verify information obtained directly through teacher questionnaires. Since the impressions collected from such visits are for general guidance rather than for detailed comparative analysis, the problem of agreement among the project's several classroom visitors is not a particularly serious one. However, particularly at the start of the visiting period, staff members who will be visiting schools should discuss their expectations and their observations with each other, thereby increasing sensitivity to clues that might otherwise be overlooked. Also, if, during the year, one visitor picks up information on some material or process causing problems in any of the schools he has visited, he may want to alert the others to this, so that they may check the extent of the problems or how the situation is handled elsewhere.

Structured Observations

Still another type of evaluative visit to the classroom is the structured observation, to accumulate data to be handled statistically.[1] The visitor may be a trained staff member or an outside specialist in the specific observation technique to be used. (Rigorous training in the technique is important, and independent observers should achieve a close agreement in their recording.) Appropriate techniques might include recording teacher-student interaction and various measures of classroom climate and activity. Through analysis of the questioning technique of the teacher, the proportion of time the teacher talks, the number and kinds of student interactions, and the number of students participating in the interaction, it is possible to describe verbal and nonverbal classroom behavior in relatively precise terms. It is also possible to determine whether the interaction pattern in the classroom is compatible with the project objectives. For example, if the analysis of classroom operation indicates that the teacher talks two-thirds of the time (not an unusually high percentage), or that the questions asked by the teacher permit only one specific correct answer, one could conclude that this is incompatible with a project objective concerned with the development of divergent thinking—thinking where the child explores new ideas and possibilities rather than focuses on a single, often previously learned, stratagem.

One can study whether the style of teaching in the classroom has changed from that used with earlier curricula or prior to the teacher

---

[1]Boyd and DeVault (1966) include an annotated bibliography and comparison of some instruments currently available for such observation. Also see Medley and Mitzel (1963) for uses, instruments, and strategies of observation.

attendance at a workshop or institute. Thus, if the project is concerned with pupil development of analytical skills and the classroom observation record indicates that teacher handling of materials both before and after the institute puts a premium on memory skills, the effectiveness of the training, as preparation for that curriculum, is questionable.

The Individually Prescribed Instruction project, concerned with changing the classroom activities of students, prepared its own student observation form (Table 3), which presents some precise descriptive data on what individuals and classes are doing and permits comparisons among pupils in one or more classes, groups in the same subject area, the same individual or group in different subject areas, groups under control and experimental conditions, and individuals and groups at different grade levels (Yeager and Lindvall, 1967). Although preparation and use of such observation forms may seem relatively simple, they require planning, tryout, redesigning, and retesting before the forms include the desired information and can be used in a uniform manner by different observers. Training observers to achieve a high degree of *reliability* or congruence in observations requires supervised practice in use of the system, along with a clear understanding of what each category means (and does not mean) and of how observations are to be made. Furthermore, from time to time during the period of observing, the observers should check to be sure that the congruence in observation is maintained.

Visits for Test Feedback

A different kind of classroom visit can be scheduled when the project has a formal testing program. The visitor may be working with one student at a time, with two or three in a small group, or with the class as a whole. Although the procedure he uses and the information garnered will vary, the purpose is to find out how the students arrived at the answer they chose for each test question and why they discarded the alternative answers. This can help explain *why* the students did well or poorly, whereas the data themselves merely indicate that a correct or incorrect answer was chosen. Using a tape recorder during such visits is strongly recommended, since, if the visitor is busy writing, he may distract the students, particularly in the individual or small group situation.

The interviewer may find that pupil difficulty with test questions arises from lack of understanding of an idea, misconceptions, lack of intellectual skills, poor wording of the questions, hasty classroom treatment of the subject, or lack of such prerequisite skills as graph and map reading. The student may suggest changes in wording that will make a question less ambiguous; for example, "If you would just add the word 'white' before 'substances,' I would see right off what you mean." The interviewer may find that students have chosen the correct answer for irrelevant reasons; for example, "The other answers were silly," or "Whenever words like 'biome' or 'ecosystem' or other broad terms are used, that is the correct answer, because the authors are always talking about those things," or "I didn't know the right answer but I could reason out that the others couldn't be right."

For individual or small group interviews, it is suggested that this technique be used with a pilot group or in lieu of classroom use of the test; for classes as a whole, it may be done the day following testing, when test papers are returned. In either case, a half-dozen interviews will often provide the feedback needed to explain test inadequacies and identify curriculum problems, provided this is supplementary to detailed statistical analyses of the test.[2] Without such direct feedback, writers may spend hours guessing why performance turned out as it did, without ever hitting on the right reason.

TEACHER FEEDBACK

Teachers using project materials on a trial basis may be asked to write frequent periodic reports reacting to the new course materials, perhaps weekly or at the end of each chapter or unit; if too much time elapses between reports, the job to be done will be lengthy and teachers may be discouraged. Some projects request structured reports and provide a checklist. Others prefer open-ended reports, since, through an oversight, the checklist may omit some important facet of concern to the teacher; even though the teacher may be invited to write comments on the reverse side of a checklist, he may feel that if the idea he has in mind were really important, it would have been included on the checklist, and so he may omit it or play it down.

For open-ended reports, there may be a tendency on the part of some teachers to be overly general, to comment merely that the materials "need improvement." In such situations the writers have no way of telling what is right or wrong with a given exercise or section unless the criticism is specific. For example, "This is good because the instructions are clear enough for students to follow in mastering a new skill"; or "Students did well till they came to Step 4, where the whole exercise

---

[2]See Table 5 pp. 93–94, illustration in the text pp. 95–96, and Appendix E for types of test data that can be useful and the interpretations that can be made from these.

TABLE 3

EXAMPLE OF DATA OBTAINED FROM
A CLASS OBSERVATION SHEET

*Mean per cent of students in grade 2 engaged in various
instructional activities at a given time*

		Math		Reading	
		Exper. %	Replica. %	Exper. %	Replica. %
I.	Independent Work	53.82	46.30	59.66	56.26
	A. The student is reading independently	1.84	4.52	.26	9.83
	B. The student is working independently on a work sheet	38.03	24.21	34.95	39.50
	C. The student is individually listening to a tape recorder				
	D. The student is independently viewing a film strip				
	E. The student is independently checking his work	.79	.96	1.77	1.35
	F. The student is working with a language master				
	G. The student is working with a disc-phonograph			22.27	
	H. The student is using programmed material				
	I. The pupil corrects a test (makes corrections)	.13			
	J. The pupil takes an individual test	2.10	12.97	.13	.58
	K. The pupil makes corrections on study exercise	3.68	2.88		3.28
	L. The pupil works with supplemental reading material			.26	
	M. The pupil makes corrections on test	1.84			
	N. Miscellaneous	5.40	.77		1.74
II.	Teacher-Pupil Work	11.05	16.14	12.09	12.53
	A. The pupil seeks assistance from the teacher	3.82	9.22	5.65	5.01
	B. The pupil receives assistance from the teacher	7.24	6.92	6.44	7.51
	C. The pupil discusses his progress with a teacher				

(TABLE 3 Cont.)

	Math		Reading	
	Exper. %	Replica. %	Exper. %	Replica. %
III. Non-Instructional Use of Pupil Time	32.89	36.98	26.54	27.55
A. Pupil spends time at desk not working	11.58	8.55	7.36	12.72
B. Pupil waits for teacher or clerk to provide lesson materials for him	.13	.19	.26	
C. Pupil waits for prescription	.66		1.05	
D. Pupil goes to get materials	3.68	2.59	7.10	1.74
E. Pupil waits for papers to be corrected by a clerk	8.42	11.24	4.47	5.39
F. Pupil talks to other pupils	5.92	3.17	5.39	5.01
G. Pupil leaves room to get material	2.50	11.24	.92	1.16
H. Miscellaneous				1.54
IV. Pupil-Pupil Activity	2.24		1.71	.19
A. Pupil asks assistance from another pupil	1.05		.92	
B. Pupil receives assistance from another pupil	1.18		.79	.19
V. Group Activity				3.48
A. The pupil contributes to a group discussion				
B. The pupil takes a group test under supervision				
C. The pupil answers a question directed to him				.19
D. The pupil asks a question				.97
E. The pupil listens to a teacher lecture or demonstrate				
F. The pupil watches a film with the group				
G. The pupil listens to records with the group				
H. The pupil watches a performance with the group				2.31

Source: John L. Yeager and C. M. Lindvall. Evaluating an instructional innovation through the observation of pupil activities. Paper presented at American Educational Research Association meeting, Chicago, February, 1967. The research and development were performed under provisions of the Cooperative Research Program.

bogged down, perhaps because the students could not be sure what was expected of them"; or "This does not work because it is too long for the class period and cannot effectively be carried over into a second day."

Part of the difficulty in obtaining precise and useful feedbâck from teachers may result from the project's reaction to the initial teacher reports. It is important that these reports be read, and that teachers know they are read. This does not mean that every suggested modification must be made, but unless the project is willing to consider suggestions from all sources with the same degree of open-mindedness, requests for teacher suggestions will build resentment rather than rapport. If the project is defensive or implies that if the teacher really understood his subject matter he would not make stupid criticisms, the teacher will soon get the message and his feedback, if it continues at all, will consist of meaningless platitudes and generalizations. Thus, unless a project genuinely wants teacher reviews and can afford the time to read these objectively, it would be well-advised not to request them.

One of the highly useful evaluative devices initiated by PSSC and adopted by a number of other projects is the *cluster* concept for obtaining reactions from teachers. During the period of classroom tryout of experimental editions of materials, the participating teachers are organized in geographic clusters or centers. Each center has a leader, selected either by the teachers or by the project. Center meetings are held at regular intervals: for some projects, this is weekly; for others, less frequently. At the center meetings, teachers talk over the work for the coming weeks and also review the work of the previous week or unit, and a report of this discussion is sent to the project. Although these teachers may already have written individual reports, the center meeting reports generally add a new dimension. While such center meetings are expensive in terms of the teacher time involved, they are highly effective in providing evaluative information, in providing in-service training, and in providing a strong supportive atmosphere for the teacher-innovators (A. Grobman, in press).

Toward the end of the school tryout year for an experimental edition of project materials, several projects have had a panel of project writers meet for several days with a group of selected teachers from a variety of school situations, to go over the teacher experiences, problems, and suggestions. While this is somewhat similar to the center meeting, in the course of the teacher-writer dialogue, ideas and solutions often arise that have not been thought of earlier. At these meetings teachers may feel in a stronger position to criticize, since they have other teachers to back them up, and, because of the variety of schools represented, it may be more possible for writers to judge whether the problems discussed arise from the materials or from factors in a given school. One low-budget project has found such meetings so successful that these have become the major item in the evaluation budget.

QUESTIONNAIRES

Many things can be learned from questionnaires completed by teachers, principals, students, parents, and experts in the subject area. They do, however, have limitations. Perhaps because questionnaires seem such an obviously easy way to collect information, they may be prepared too casually. There is often an overreliance on them, and, in all too many instances, the investigator does not realize the limitations and possibly misleading implications of his questionnaire data.

People in the questionnaire sample may be deluged with questionnaires, many of them inappropriate for the persons being questioned. The respondent may not answer or may give casual responses simply because he is tired of questionnaires. The questions may be phrased to make accurate answering difficult. Filling out some questionnaires requires mastery of a complicated answering system.

Each question and the questionnaire as a whole should be tried out in advance, to determine whether they elicit the information desired by the project; a question meaning one thing to the investigator may mean something very different to the respondent. One project's question concerning length of teaching experience of project participants had overlapping categories, so that Option A was "1 to 5 years" and Option B was "5 to 10 years." Another project asked the number of collegiate credits in science, evidently to determine the subject matter mastery of its experimental teachers. Some teachers answered in semester hours, some in trimester hours, and some lumped these together. Furthermore, there was no way of distinguishing in the responses between three graduate hours in genetics or astrophysics on the one hand, and three credits of health for physical education majors or preparing audio-visual aids for elementary science on the other.

In an attempt to tie down the background factors that excellent teachers have in common, one project sent questionnaires to a list of teachers identified as excellent by experts. The major information garnered was that good teachers in that particular subject area are males over forty from rural backgrounds. In planning the questionnaire, the investigator completely overlooked the bias in sample selection. The experts he chose knew few young people because their contacts were largely through professional societies, and so the recommendations were based primarily on the number of offices held in such societies, positions that rarely fall to younger members. As a rule, men are more free to attend professional meetings, since women may have more family responsibilities. And most adults living in cities today did not grow up in cities. Insofar as their reasons for becoming teachers were concerned, the respondents chose high-sounding platitudes, when, in fact, many would privately admit that during the depression years when they entered teaching, it was the only way to earn a steady income. In an attempt to obtain data from other teachers, to make comparisons with the so-called exemplary groups, the project sent out a second letter, omitting the sentence indicating that the teachers had been selected as exemplary. A number of persons in this second group compared notes with those receiving the more complimentary letter, and project goodwill suffered a considerable and unnecessary blow.

To get reactions from experts in science education, one evaluator sampled the mailing lists of some of the professional societies in this field; thus, the questionnaire went not only to subject matter specialists but also to some high school and college students. Since responses to the questionnaires were anonymous, there was no way of telling which came from experts and which from nonexperts. Even when just experts answer, some will give their views without ever seeing the materials, perhaps because they do not want to admit this. Ten carefully written reviews from selected experts are worth far more for evaluative purposes than several thousand such questionnaire responses.

If large numbers of questionnaires are to be used, advance consideration of the problems of layout, in order to facilitate transfer of data for machine processing, can significantly increase accuracy of data transfer and save money and time. In questioning students, one project had students give questionnaire answers directly on standard IBM answer sheets, thereby obviating the need for transfer of the data from questionnaire schedules to data cards. It may be helpful to have questionnaires printed in reduced type, thereby condensing the form and making them look less formidable. A review of several books dealing with the preparation of questionnaires (e.g., Rummell, 1964; Selltiz *et al.*, 1966; Backstrom and Hursh, 1963; Oppenheimer, 1966), and, when possible, a check with someone experienced in questionnaire strategies, is well worth the effort, even for a seemingly simple questionnaire.

THE SMALL-SCALE TRYOUT

A number of projects have set up various kinds of simulated situations for trying out materials. Several have used computers programmed for individual student use, with a detailed record kept of student successes and failures. One science study had two high school teachers on duty in a high school science laboratory for the duration of the project summer writing conference. Their task was to try out all new laboratory experiments as they were written, to determine whether these were workable, and also to try alternate ways of performing the experiments using various chemicals and instruments to determine optimal suitability for achieving the desired skills.

Some projects have rosters of *instant students* or *instant classes* of a specific kind, available on short notice to try out ideas or materials as they are developed. During one of its summer writing conferences, the BSCS hired about a dozen high school students for several hours each morning to work in a nearby high school trying out course materials as they were written. At times the tryout materials were laboratory exercises or parts of laboratory exercises; at other times text or discussion materials or tests were involved. The writers of the portion being tested on a given day would usually visit the classroom during or after the trial to discuss the activity with the students and teachers. The kinds of questions these formative evaluation activities answered with some degree of success concerned clarity of instructions, time required for various activities, adequacy of prerequisite knowledge, difficulty level, and whether the point of the activity was coming through at all.

Similar small-scale tryouts, using just a few students or classes, have been used by other projects during the school year for a variety of purposes: to develop alternate sequences; to try something so different from conventional curricula that the writers want a small tryout before exposing large numbers of students; when one unit or activity in the experimental year has not worked well, and the writers want early feedback on a revised version of the same activity or unit; or for special micro-evaluation studies of a particular facet of the curriculum.

TESTS[3]

Perhaps the written test is the most frequently used device in systematic evaluations. But written tests, as they are generally conceived, represent only a limited facet of the possibilities of testing. Tests may be written or oral. They may require selection from a group of answers or may require the student to supply his own answer. The test may be programmed, where the selection of the first answer determines the order of presentation of the following questions, and there may be an automatic record made of the order in which questions are answered

[3]The word *tests* is used here to include achievement tests as well as attitude and personality scales.

or answers chosen. (See McGuire, 1968 for illustration of this technique.) The test may require the student to perform some task, as in a laboratory practical or a swimming test. He may be asked to write answers or to give oral answers. The questions may be written or presented orally, through pictures, a situation, a movie, or a computer or other programmed device. One major limit of tests is that they measure only what the student can do or is willing to do in the testing situation; they do not necessarily measure what he will do in an out-of-test situation. Thus, a road test in driving may measure ability to obey driving regulations; it does not mean that these regulations will be obeyed out of the testing situation. Nonetheless, such a performance test is probably a better predictor than a pencil-and-paper test that asks about a law concerning right-of-way or stop signs.

Subject matter tests are most often limited to measuring knowledge and the ability to apply this knowledge in situations similar to those studied, as for example, the recall of a mathematical formula and the ability to apply the formula to a problem similar to those worked earlier. But subject matter tests need not be so limited. Even in testing relatively large numbers of students, it is possible to measure more complex cognitive skills. Creative ability, problem-solving ability, values, attitudes, and interests are all measurable, at least to some extent, through written tests.

Generally more attention is given to the selection and scoring of a test than to the administration of the test to the subjects, an oversight that can seriously bias data with no possibility of later identification of the bias or compensation for it. The detail to which instructions may be standardized is illustrated in Kropp and Stoker (1966) and is well worth emulating.

CRITERIA FOR SELECTION OR CONSTRUCTION OF TESTS

> . . . if we start with a wrong assumption no amount of energy and ingenuity in the manipulation of scientific technique will convert this initial error into a sound principal.
>
> Boyd H. Bode (1927)

One might assume that it would be relatively simple to select an existing test to measure the abilities and skills a curriculum project is concerned with. This is the case insofar as measures of general ability are concerned, and most projects will need such a test to describe the student group using its materials and to permit statistical comparisons among students or among groups. There are also some existing achievement tests that may be useful to some projects. For example, in measuring reading readiness (the readiness of the young child to learn to read) or in measuring reading ability at the end of the first or second grade, there are a number of tests that are reasonably suitable for many situations. (There are some questions concerning the validity of many of these tests for some cultural groups, including the disadvantaged or those for whom English is a second language.) In most cases, however, projects will have difficulty finding suitable achievement and attitude tests to measure some facets of their concern. Developing a new test is still more difficult, but it may be necessary. In the choice of an existing test or in the development of a new one, suitability to the curriculum and the test population are of paramount importance.

Validity

Validity is concerned with relevance—with the extent to which the test is relevant to the purposes for which it is being used.[4] Validity exists only in terms of a particular context, and the context for which an existing test was developed may be quite different from that of the project. For example, all mathematics tests measure some mathematics-related skills, but the skills a test measures may not be those a curriculum project is concerned with. It is important to keep in mind that if published tests are intended for broad use, they must reflect existing curricula in general use. If a curriculum project is established because the existing emphasis in history teaching has been inadequate in terms of subject coverage, organization, materials, and skills taught, then a history test reflecting such existing curricula is inappropriate for measuring student achievement of different coverage, organization of materials, and skills.

In chemistry, both CHEM Study and CBA selected materials and ideas that were radically different from those in previous high school chemistry books and also radically different from each other. Thus, even a test developed for one new curriculum might not be suitable for students in another, unless it focuses on knowledge and skills common to both, or unless it is subject-matter free—that is, it provides all the factual information needed by the student—and measures skills relevant to both. Thus, a test of critical thinking, such as the Cornell Test

---

[4]French and Michael (1966) include a useful detailed discussion of content validity, criterion-related validity, construct validity, and reliability, all of which are of vital concern in testing.

of Critical Thinking (Ennis, 1961) or the Watson-Glazer Test of Critical Thinking (Watson and Glazer, 1964), might be used in any chemistry curriculum in which the development of critical thinking is an aim. However, the fact that a test measures critical thinking does not mean that the test author's definition of critical thinking is the same as that of the curriculum project or even of another test writer. At question is not only the intent of the test writer as stated in the manual accompanying the test but also the degree to which he implements this stated intent. (Often test users accept without question the test author's stated purpose, even though they would judge a textbook not by the author's foreword but by the contents of the book itself.)

Some have argued that as long as a test includes materials covered by a new curriculum, it is appropriate for evaluation of the curriculum and of performance of students in that curriculum. Others judge appropriateness of a test by student scores on the test. Thus, if students in a new curriculum are not penalized in their test performance (when compared with students in other curricula), the test would be considered appropriate. This is the reasoning followed in the College Entrance Examination Board statement (CEEB, 1967) concerning BSCS, CHEM Study, and PSSC students on the CEEB examinations in biology, chemistry, and physics offered in December 1966, when it states that "Since the differences are small . . . and since half of the differences favor the newer curriculums and half favor the more traditional curriculums, it can be concluded that the three science Achievement Tests are equally appropriate for students of the more traditional and students of the newer curriculums in high school science."

Such reasoning ignores two considerations. First, the test may give an inappropriate emphasis to some portions of the new curriculum and minimize or even exclude other major areas; in such a case, the test would not have content validity, since it would not accurately reflect the course or the desired learnings by students. Second, whether or not they are intended as such, tests are teaching devices and thereby constitute an integral part of the curriculum. They provide students and teachers with verification of the intent of the curriculum. Through long exposure, students have become accustomed to courses that urge thinking and reasoning but that reward recall of minutiae on the tests; many tests merely reinforce this experience. Thus, even if students in the experimental curriculum can handle the items in a test, its use may distort the students' perception of the course and so make the curriculum less effective.

In research studies designed to describe differences in learnings between students in the new curriculum and students in the one it replaced, it may be appropriate to use tests reflecting neither the content nor the aims of the project's curriculum. Here, low scores of experimental students would not be a matter of concern. For example, in 1961–62, when the BSCS used the then_current 1948 edition of the Cooperative Biology Test with groups of students in its evaluation program, the staff interpreted high student scores as indicating that some teachers were including too much traditional biology in their BSCS courses. A one-time testing of this type may not adversely affect the experimental program if the test to be used has not been announced in advance (so there is no change in teaching to reflect the emphasis on the test), if teachers are informed why this test is being used, and if students understand that their grades will not be affected by scores on this test. However, if there is frequent use of tests that do not reflect the aims of the new program, teachers and students develop values concerning the program and the relative importance of its various aspects that may be highly detrimental to future teaching and learning.

Test Grids

Although it is easy to suggest that each test or battery (or series) of tests used in the evaluation program reflect the intended emphasis of the curriculum, it may be difficult to make a systematic judgment of appropriateness. A completely unsuitable test may not be difficult to spot; but the lack of appropriateness of an achievement test that tends to deal with the subject coverage of the new curriculum may not be as obvious.

Two of the problems in systematically scrutinizing tests or in constructing new tests are balance among subject areas and balance among cognitive skills. As a solution, some kind of *test grid*, or test plan, is useful. Such grids represent attempts to permit systematic and objective analysis of tests, to determine in precise terms the subject coverage and skills required of the student. While generally no single test or evaluation instrument will provide coverage of all facets of the project's aims, the totality of the evaluation efforts should provide at least some evidence on most of the major facets of these aims. Often, the test grid will have two axes, one for content coverage and the other for cognitive skills being tested. (See Table 4.) This is particularly useful in analyzing a single test; further, with different colors of ink indicating different tests, several tests can be compared or cumulated on one grid. A different type of grid (see Figure 1) may be more useful in comparing several tests.

With practice, users of the test grid can achieve reasonably high agreement on assignment of test questions to categories (Easley *et al.*,

TABLE 4

GENERAL GRID FORM DEVELOPED BY BSCS, ADAPTED
FOR USE WITH BSCS SECOND COURSE MATERIALS

BIOLOGICAL SCIENCES CURRICULUM STUDY

SECOND COURSE TEST GRID

	Biological themes							Sciences as inquiry										Intell. history	Totals
	Evolution	Diversity of type & unity of pattern	Genetic continuity	Complem. of org. & environment	Biol. roots of behavior	Comp. of structure & function	Homeostasis and regulation	Use of scientific literature	Interpret qualitative data	Interpret quantitative data	Analysis of data with statistics	Unstd. relev. of data to problem	Judge design of expt's.	Screen hypotheses	Identify problems	Apply principles of inquiry	Analyze scientific reports		
A. Ability to recall & reorganize materials learned																			
1-1 Terminology																			
1-2 Specific facts																			
2-1 Conventions																			
2-2 Trends and sequences																			
2-3 Classifications and categories																			
2-4 Criteria																			
2-5 Methodology																			
3-1 Principles and generalizations																			
3-2 Theories and structures																			

B. Ability to apply knowledge to new concrete situations
1 Non-quantitative knowledge
2 Quantitative materials

C. Ability to use skills involved in understanding scientific problems
0 Use of scientific literature
1-1 Interpret qualitative data
1-2 Interpret quantitative data
1-3 Appl. of statistical tech. to data
2 Undstd. relev. of data to problem
3 Screen and judge design of expt's
4 Screen hypotheses
5 Identify problems
6 Identify & apply prin. of inquiry
7 Analyze scientific reports

D. Ability to show relationships between bodies of knowledge
1 Comparison
2 Extrapolation
3-1 Application—to another biol. area
3-2 Application—to other fields
4 Analysis of relationships
5 Interrelate facts, prins. in a new way
6 Development of new interrelated concepts

Totals

Source: Biological Sciences Curriculum Study. Reproduced with permission. For explanation of categories on the vertical axis, see Klinckmann (1963).

FIGURE 1

EASLEY-KENDZIOR-WALLACE GRID FOR COMPARISON
OF EMPHASES AMONG TESTS

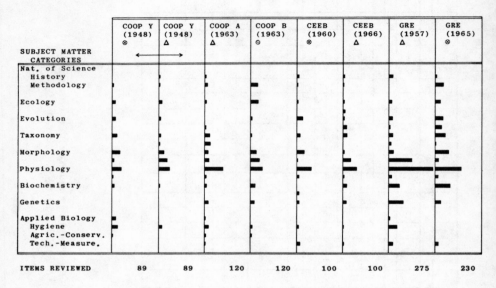

ITEMS REVIEWED   89   89   120   120   100   100   275   230

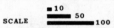

SCALE

KEY

Tests analyzed

COOP Y (1948) Cooperative Biology Test (Form Y), Test Number 624-
84-1 (1948), Educational Testing Service: Part I, 55 items, 20 minutes;
Part II, 34 items, 20 minutes.

COOP A (1963) Cooperative Science Tests (Form A) Biology, Educational
Testing Service: Part I, 60 items, 40 minutes;   Part II, 60 items,40
minutes.

COOP B (1963) Cooperative Science Tests (Form B) Biology, Educational
Testing Service: Part I, 60 items, 40 minutes; Part II, 60 items, 40 mins.

CEEB (1960) College Entrance Examination Board, Achievement Test,
Biology, Form 1 AC (1960), Educational Testing Service: 100 items.

CEEB (1966) College Entrance Examination Board, Achievement Test,
Biology, Form O AC2 (1966), Educational Testing Service: 100 items.

(FIGURE 1 Cont.)

KNOWLEDGE FORMS	COOP Y (1948) ⊗	COOP Y (1948) Δ	COOP A (1963) Δ	COOP B (1963) ⊙	CEEB (1960) ⊗	CEEB (1966) Δ	GRE (1957) Δ	GRE (1965) ⊗
Definition								
Fact								
Principle								
Interpr. of Data	*	*						

ANSWERING PROCESSES	COOP Y (1948) ⊗	COOP Y (1948) Δ	COOP A (1963) Δ	COOP B (1963) ⊙	CEEB (1960) ⊗	CEEB (1966) Δ	GRE (1957) Δ	GRE (1965) ⊗
Recall								
Deduction								
Reasoning								
Guess								

ITEMS REVIEWED	89	89	120	120	100	100	275	230
DISPUTED ITEMS	8	8	6	1	0	0	2	6

* majority are
  reading comprehension

SCALE ▪ 10 ▬ 50 ▬▬ 100

(KEY Cont.)

GRE (1957) The Graduate Record Examinations, Advanced Tests, Biology Form FGR 24 Booklet 013-R7 (1956) 1957, Educational Testing Service: 275 items, 3 hours.

GRE (1965) The Graduate Record Examinations, Advanced Tests, Biology Form NGR-2 Booklet, Educational Testing Service: 230 items, 3 hours.

Test analyst—Symbols are used to identify the test analyst as follows:

⊙ refers to analyst with predisposition toward classical morphology and taxonomy.

Δ refers to analyst with predisposition toward microbiology and biochemistry.

⊗ refers to analyst with predisposition toward genetics, ecology, and evolution.

Source: J. A. Easley, Jr., Elizabeth Kendzior, Robert Wallace. A 'bio-assay' of biology tests. *The American Biology Teacher*, May, 1967. Reproduced with permission of the publisher.

1967); disagreements are generally within a broad category, for example within category C in Table 4 rather than between categories B and C.

The usefulness of a grid is indicated by the experience of one project whose evaluation for several years had depended almost entirely on student achievement on a single, standardized test relevant to the subject area. The project had not been sympathetic to numerous criticisms of the test by experimental schools; however, when project personnel analyzed the test through use of a grid, they realized that at least half of the items demanded recall, and it was on these rather than on items involving higher cognitive skills, that students did poorly.

The novice using a grid may confuse complexity and mental (cognitive) process involved; these are quite different. Often, when a question is buried in a difficult reading passage, it will appear to require a high level of reasoning, perhaps synthesis or analysis skills, whereas once the reading task has been accomplished, the test item is only a what-is-it or how-does-it-work question, requiring recall or direct application of recalled fact. Another difficulty in gridding tests is that one must be familiar with the curriculum materials being tested and, for strictest accuracy, with the classroom activities of the students; for example, a question that requires synthesis or analysis for one curriculum or class may require only recall for others, since it may refer to a situation considered in the latter class but not in the former one.

The test grid used by a project must be tailored to that project, so that the grid includes areas and skills of project concern. It should also provide for areas the project may not be concerned with but that may appear on its own tests or on outside tests being checked for appropriateness. For example, the BSCS experienced difficulties in using its grid for analysis of outside tests, since its categories did not precisely fit some of the test items being analyzed; thus, although items were assigned to the best category available, this did not accurately reflect the external test (Klinckmann, 1963). Work with the grid by project personnel can pay off in terms of helping them to clarify the aims of the project; further, it can help them to understand the limitations of objective tests and the need to develop a broader concept of evaluation.

Other important technical aspects in test selection are listed in *Standards for educational and psychological tests* (French and Michael, 1966). While new project tests and many unpublished tests cannot be expected to meet many of these criteria, these are limitations that should be kept in mind in their use.

Reading Level

Another problem in test selection is reading level, that is, the difficulty of vocabulary, the complexity and length of sentences, and the total amount of reading. The fact that a test is published and standardized does not necessarily mean that the reading level is suitable for the students being tested or even for the average student at that grade level. One student, after struggling almost to the point of tears over the first page of a standardized social studies test used to evaluate a new curriculum, said plaintively to the test administrator, "If you will just tell me what the questions are, I'll be glad to answer, but I don't know what you're asking." The reading level of this test was above the average for the grade level in which it was being used, and test scores for many students merely reflected their ability or inability to work through some highly intricate sentences to locate the routine factual questions being asked.

A test written at *grade level* (that is, average level of the group) for an unselected group of students will be above the measured reading ability of half the group. Unless a test is specifically intended to measure reading skills, some evaluators have suggested that the test be written at least one and possibly two years below the average reading level for the grade at which it is being used.

Oversimplification

In some instances attempts to simplify the reading level of a test may result in wording that communicates misinformation; some items (test questions) seem impossible to simplify without sacrificing accuracy. In such cases, it is far better to delete an item from the test or not use the test in which it appears. For example, in one general science test, a question tried to get at the idea that for the most part, trees will die if they are flooded for any length of time. To keep the question brief and simple, no allowance was made for students familiar with mangrove and cypress trees, the normal habitat of which is standing water. Such students would be penalized for having this extra information; further, the test taught students the misinformation that all trees in standing water will die. One can rationalize that only a few students are penalized for overlearning (knowing more than is expected of them) and that other students have the test only briefly and are too busy answering questions to learn much new information. Such a hope hardly excuses presenting incorrect information and penalizing students who use direct experience to answer test questions.

Cultural Bias

There may be special problems of cultural bias in tests insofar as students in the project's audience are concerned. Such bias may be most obvious in the picture tests often used with children who have not learned to read well; here, the teacher reads a question, and the child answers by selecting from among several pictures in the test booklet. Objects are often shown that children in some economic, social, or geographic groups will not recognize, and such lack of familiarity may be unrelated to content or skills the project is trying to measure. For example, in one such test in the social studies, a furnace is pictured. For millions of children, this is as familiar an object as a house or a shoe; however, for children living in Hawaii, Southern California, Florida, or in an apartment complex elsewhere, this is an entirely strange object, and the question is therefore inappropriate *in terms of the intended purpose.* The test author was probably thinking of objects that he was familiar with as a child or that his own children, living in a small Northern college community, are familiar with; he obviously had not questioned the universality of such knowledge for today's child.

There is also a more invidious kind of cultural bias. Although various curriculum projects may not state in their objectives that they wish to avoid contributing to antisocial prejudices or social hostility, they certainly would espouse such an objective. Yet they may inadvertently select tests that heighten such negative feelings. For example, in one picture test, all pictures of professional people and businessmen are clearly identifiable as blond Caucasians, while all custodial personnel are Negroes. Projects that would clearly reject such an overt statement may not notice the implications of these pictures. Such bias is not limited to picture tests. In one economics test, two of the test's fifty items deal with unions, and in both of these, the connotation is entirely unfavorable.

Difficulty Level

One set of tests may serve three purposes: to determine the extent of student mastery of skills, to convey to student and teacher what is important in the curriculum, and to serve as a basis for grades. If a test is to be multipurpose, it may have to fit a pattern different from that of the standardized test used primarily to separate students along a continuum. Some psychometricians (specialists in psychological measurement) suggest that tests should have an average difficulty level of

50 per cent; that is, the average student scores should be half of the items correct. They further recommend that individual questions be at different levels of difficulty but that no extremely easy questions—questions almost everyone gets correct—be included. If the purpose of a project test is to find out how much of the curriculum students have mastered, a 50 per cent level of achievement may unduly limit the feedback on the extent of student successes. It also tends to discourage students and disaffect teachers and parents who are used to higher grades. It does little good to explain that a score of 50 per cent is C or average; they do not believe it, and their negative reactions to lower scores may be quite serious in terms of project rapport and student progress.

Contrary to usual test practice, the project may want to include in its test some items that virtually everyone gets correct, since these may deal with *threshold skills*, skills that all students should master before going on. Just because most students have probably mastered them does not mean that a check is unnecessary. In a laboratory course, unless a student can focus the microscope with some degree of success, he cannot profitably proceed with microscope experiments. In the first grade, if a child does not know the difference between a red light and a green light, he cannot be permitted to cross the street alone. These are basic, prerequisite skills, and 50 per cent of the students mastering them is not enough.

LOCATING EXISTING TESTS

The standard source on published tests, the *Mental measurements yearbook* series (Buros, 1965), issued at five-year intervals, lists the source of each test, what it purports to measure, length of the test, grade level, and, most valuable of all, two critical, carefully prepared reviews by testing experts. Without doubt, these reviews are worth reading before using any of the listed tests. Although the nonpsychologist may find some of the terminology in the reviews obscure, he can still find out what the experts think the test measures and what the limitations of the tests are. The *Yearbook* does not include tests prepared for specific materials (for a given textbook, for example), therefore some of the tests developed by curriculum projects are not included. *Tests in print* (Buros, 1961) is helpful in supplementing the *Yearbook;* it includes some tests, such as research instruments that are not included in the *Yearbook*. A new series edited by Buros, the *Mental measurements yearbook monograph series*, will include a broader variety of tests; the first in the series is *Reading tests and reviews* (Buros, 1968), and the second will deal with science tests (Buros, in preparation).

For atttiude scales, Shaw and Wright's *Scales for measurement of attitudes* (1967) and Lake and Miles's *The assessment of social functioning* (forthcoming) include unpublished attitude scales thereby providing listings different from the *Yearbook*. *Psychological abstracts*, a periodic reference series, includes information on new tests. Carl Campbell Brigham Library of Educational Testing Service[5] is developing a comprehensive collection of educational and psychological tests. Some education and psychology journals review tests regularly, but the coverage may not include the areas of concern to the curriculum project.

Likely sources for checking on the existence of useful unpublished tests include the new bibliography service of University Microfilms Library Services.[6] Another source is the ERIC Center[7] for the pertinent subject area, such as education of the disadvantaged or science education. (This is also a good source for reports of research done by other projects.) Programs of recent meetings of the American Psychological Association, the American Educational Research Association, and the National Council for Measurement in Education frequently identify new tests that are the bases of research papers.[8]

Other curriculum projects in the same general field, or even in different subject areas or grade levels, may provide tests that can be adopted or adapted by another project. For example, the Science Process Inventory used by Harvard Project Physics (Welch, 1966) appears relevant to any physical science curriculum; with slight modification (substitution of the word *chemistry* or *biology* for *physics*) of many items, it might well be appropriate in the other areas of high school science.

---

[5]Princeton, N. J. 08540. This library also issues a bimonthly newsletter listing new tests received.

[6]University Microfilms Library Services, Ann Arbor, Michigan, 48106, which maintains copies of masters and doctoral dissertations from most American universities and indexes them by subject, provides, at a small charge, bibliographies of dissertations dealing with a particular subject. This may aid in retrieval of unpublished tests, provided the test is identified in the title of the study.

[7]ERIC is a recently established system for retrieval of research information in education. The Central ERIC is in the U.S. Office of Education, Washington, D.C., and there is a network of clearinghouses throughout the country, each responsible for information in a given area of education. Each clearinghouse is collecting records and studies not available through regular publication channels and is making them available through a Document Reproduction Service.

[8]See also Information storage, retrieval and dissemination. *Educational researcher*, Supplement, 1967 (American Educational Research Association), for further sources to investigate.

DEVELOPING NEW TESTS AND
OTHER MEASUREMENT INSTRUMENTS[9]

Any time an existing test comes close to meeting the evaluation need, it is far more efficient to use it as is, or to modify it, than to build a new instrument. Nonetheless, sooner or later most projects will probably have to build some kind of test.

The figure of $250 has been cited by one testing agency as a conservative estimate of the cost of developing a single test item. On this basis, a fifty-item standardized objective test would cost $12,500. Such a test differs from one written by the teacher the night before giving it to his class because the latter is not able to deal with such concerns as imbalance among areas and skills tested, reading level of items, ambiguity of questions, multiple correct answers to a question or no really correct answer, answers that are given away through use of leading words or ridiculous wrong alternatives, the inadequate range of difficulty of items, and insufficient data on individual items and on the test as a whole to give a check on test reliability and validity and to provide some standards of expectations in terms of achievement.

The difficulty of writing new tests is illustrated by the BSCS experience during one of its early experimental years. As part of their feedback reports, all BSCS teachers were asked to provide the BSCS with copies of their classroom tests. In this way the BSCS hoped to build a pool of good test items for its exams. From the hundreds of tests received, not a single item could be salvaged; every item submitted by teachers measured only recall or direct application of knowledge. As a group the BSCS teachers were not poor teachers; nor were they atypical in the way they prepared tests. Rather, their tests reflected lack of training in test writing,[10] lack of time to build tests, and, for many, lack of a particular talent for test writing. Project personnel, unless trained in test writing, probably would fare no better.

While an easy solution would be the hiring of good test writers, such people are scarce and generally are already busy. There is also difficulty in explaining to an outsider exactly what it is the project is aiming to do. Given detailed behavioral objectives, an outsider can write items to fit these. For most projects, however, such detailing is not immediately practical; also, if, through an oversight something

---

[9]For an annotated bibliography on test writing, see H. Grobman (1967).

[10]Even those teachers who have had collegiate Test and Measurement courses have probably not studied item writing, since measurement courses generally stress selection, use, and interpretation of standardized tests, not the preparation of classroom tests.

important is omitted from the objectives list, it would not be tested and this omission might not even be identified.

One might suggest that the professional test writer read the experimental materials and find out from these what the test coverage should be. While this can be useful, if the test is to evaluate the materials, it should reflect not only what is in the materials but also any other intent of the writers, which they may have failed to include in the materials. In fact, the latter is one of the very useful functions of test writing during the formative evaluation stage. Such omissions may be relatively minor, such as a common technical term that should have been included. Or they can be basic; for example, until it tried to prepare tests, one science project did not realize that no work on quantification skills (graph and table reading and collection and interpretation of data) appeared in the first third of the course, an omission that was unintentional and contrary to the philosophy of the course.

Another alternative is to train persons familiar with the curriculum—project staff, committee members, writers, experimental teachers—in test writing; however, there are some risks involved. On the positive side, if the training program is sound, each participant will probably emerge with a far better understanding of classroom testing and will be a better test critic; each will also come away with a clearer understanding of what he himself is trying to do in the classroom and of the appropriateness of his implementation of these aims. Many will find their teaching skills improved as a result. Some participants will become superb test writers. Some will be able to write better, but not excellent, items. But some may only improve their technical skill, so that their items, though still mundane and recall-type, are less cumbersome and ambiguous.

There is not yet a valid method for predicting which persons can be trained to become outstanding test writers. Thus, in setting up training programs for test writers, there is only a slight chance of turning out more than six or eight competent, creative writers from an initial group of eighteen to twenty participants. This does not mean that the training money is wasted, since in a well-organized program all participants will learn or refine some skills; but the project should be willing to invest in a larger group than will pay off in terms of turning out creative test writers.[11]

---

[11]A training schedule that has worked well on a number of occasions included two 3½-day sessions for all participants and a third 3½-day session for selected participants who seemed to have most promise. A by-product of this series was the production of some imaginative test items which, though they needed refining, were later used in the project's tests. It is important to recognize that inadequate staffing of such training sessions can be a serious hindrance. A 1:4 or at the very

OTHER EVALUATIVE INFORMATION

One of the problems with delimiting project objectives in advance and focusing entirely on these in the evaluation is that the project cannot anticipate all important positive and negative outcomes and it probably cannot anticipate all ways of obtaining evidence. Furthermore, for some kinds of outcomes, lack of evidence does not mean that it does not exist; the evidence simply may not come to the project's attention.

On "back-to-school night," one parent asked a teacher using experimental classroom materials, "What is going on in class? Jerry has never talked about school so much before, and to hear him, you would think he only takes this one subject." This is useful evaluation evidence. But even if children are this enthusiastic, perhaps their parents do not come to PTA; or if they do, they may not mention this enthusiasm to the teacher, or the teacher may not pass along this information to the project. Thus, this parent's comment is positive evidence supportive of the materials; lack of such a volunteered comment would not constitute negative evidence. A parent questionnaire asking whether the parent noticed any difference would not be as strong evidence as the volunteered comment, and, in some situations, might give invalid information.

One SMSG student, a seventh grader with arithmetic skills at grade level, interrupted a dinner table comment criticizing a newspaper story on average teacher salaries to ask, "Which average are they using, the mode, median, or mean? Perhaps they are just using the best one for making their case." Such an insight indicates, better than any classroom test, that this student understood quite a bit about averages and about the interpretation of data. On her own initiative, she was able to identify familiar elements in an unfamiliar situation and to bring her information to bear on it in an out-of-school context.

Another junior high school new math student complained at home that the teacher of an accelerated class in social studies insisted on grading on a curve and that this was silly, since grading on a curve was suitable only with a large, normally distributed population. (This situation was not a duplication of an example in the mathematics book.)

---

least 1:5 ratio of staff to participants seems imperative if the situation is to be optimally productive.

It is not possible to give a meaningful estimate of the cost of such training sessions, since a large part of the budget can be for travel and living expenses away from home if participants come from a wide geographic area. Another major factor is salaries or honoraria. If the participants and training staff are already on the payroll, the cost is substantially reduced.

Again, a student had taken ideas out of the context of the mathematics class and used them functionally. These are some of the very skills SMSG is interested in producing, but one could hardly predict that these two specific behaviors would be used as criterion measures for successful learning, and even if one had set up a broad objective that would cover such behaviors, that these occurrences would come to the attention of the project.

At a professional meeting, one high school principal asked a project representative about getting "the books that cut down on window breakage." Over lunch, one of his colleagues had told him that students using these new materials were not breaking as many windows. In a disadvantaged school, the principal mentioned to a visitor from the curriculum project that students who were truant generally turned up for one class during the day, a class using the experimental curriculum. Not only would this be difficult evidence to anticipate, but it might well have been modified by the principal's action if, when the students did come to school, he had disciplined them for the hours they missed. Again, in these instances the positive evidence is useful in terms of the evaluation of the materials, but lack of such behavior would not necessarily constitute failure to achieve an objective.

Some of the curriculum projects have been taking exhibit booths at professional meetings; at one such booth the frequent comment by college professors was a complaint that: "If this is what you are teaching high school students, what is left for our freshman courses?" And, "After the excitement and activity of your course, our freshmen are bored with our lectures; they want to explore ideas and do things themselves." This too is evaluation evidence worthy of note.

One index of success may be the change in college programs to reflect the different preparation and different students resulting from the new curricula, or the change in junior or senior high school programs to reflect earlier learnings. Some colleges have dropped some of their freshman science courses because they now expect entering students to have already obtained the skills previously taught in college. Some colleges consider giving Advanced Placement standing to entering students who have had project high school materials. While such outcomes were not anticipated or intended by the projects involved, they nonetheless constitute evidence that is useful in weighing the impact of these programs.

Although the projects have not specified as one of their aims the identification of promising teaching personnel and their further development and professional advancement, evidence that this has occurred is important and may in the long run have as pronounced an effect on upgrading education as do the new materials developed.

The demand by school systems for new teachers who have had special preparation to use one of the new curricula is evidence not only of acceptance of a curriculum but also of acceptance of the idea of specific teacher training appropriate to the curriculum.

The rate of adoption of the new materials is an important evaluative criterion, although caution must be used in interpretation of such data. Textbook adoption is a slow process because of fiscal problems and legal regulations.[12] Some states consider adoptions in a particular subject area only every five years. For nonadoption states, if books in use were purchased fairly recently, newer project materials, regardless of their worth, will probably not be purchased until the books on hand wear out, probably after at least four years of use.

Mere purchase of books or other materials is only a partial index of use. What is important is whether these are used or gather dust. Many schools have films, supplemental readings, maps, and microscopes that are unused. Equally important is how these are used. Much of the material and equipment is misused. Films are sometimes used only when the teacher has not prepared a lesson, or, in his absence, when it is a "safe" lesson for the substitute teacher. The field trip, recommended by the project as enrichment, may be a way of filling time at the end of the semester when the textbook is completed.

Most of the situations cited above use what Webb *et al.*, (1966) call *nonreactive measures*, measures that already exist or that are collected without the knowledge of the individual to whom the data pertain. Thus, the information is not contaminated by the individual's awareness that he is being observed for a particular purpose. While records of attendance, window breakage, truancy, library usage, and book adoptions exist for purposes other than curriculum evaluation, they can be useful in curriculum evaluation. The problem is largely one of thinking of ways in which existing records can be used.

Webb is an interesting and good source for ideas on such measures. As the project progresses and its personnel maintain sensitivity to a wide variety of feedback, other measures may be suggested on the basis of a one-time report, such as the truancy or window-breaking com-

---

[12]In such states as Texas and Florida, at certain intervals a state textbook committee adopts one or more textbooks in each subject and grade level; schools in the state are limited to such books insofar as purchases with state funds are concerned. Thus, in effect, public schools are restricted to books on the adoption list, and a 1963 edition of curriculum project materials may not legally be considered for adoption in some states until 1967 or 1968, if this is the calendar for adoptions in that subject area.

ments. Here, visiting the school and talking to teachers, pupils, other school personnel, and to parents can give useful clues; although not all such reports can be readily subjected to tests for validity, they may provide more insight into the outcomes of the curriculum than do objective test results.

Clearly, evaluative evidence can come from many sources; a listing of such sources is limited only by the imagination of the list-maker. In fact, many useful evaluative devices are not even recognized as such by their users. Thus, after scanning lists of evaluative possibilities and reports of what other persons have done,[13] the most practical procedure for a project is to be open to evaluative feedback regardless of source and regardless of whether it was anticipated in the evaluation design.

---

[13]For locating such information, check evaluation bibliographies, such as those in the monographs of the *AERA Monograph series on curriculum evaluation;* periodical indices including *Readers guide, Education index, Public affairs information service, Psychological abstracts;* the ERIC Clearinghouse service; newsletters of various curriculum studies (*BSCS Newsletters*, 19, 24, and 30 include reports of the kinds of evaluations a number of the large curriculum studies have done); and information sources referred to in Information storage, retrieval and dissemination in the *Educational researcher*, Supplement, 1967 (American Educational Research Association).

5

Arrangements

SOME CONSIDERATIONS IN BUDGETING

Evaluation does not come cheaply, but an optimal evaluation is not necessarily one in which as much money is spent as the project can figure out how to spend. Even if qualified research personnel is available, too many people doing too many different things can flood experimental classrooms with people and tests and can interfere with the classroom tryout of materials; or it can result in excessive time spent in coordinating the various efforts, with a less effective evaluation than a more modest effort would have provided.

In budgeting, perhaps the best starting point is to ask what is needed most in the way of evaluation information and at what point this is needed. Thus, it is suggested that evaluation should be planned and budgeted not one year at a time but over a longer period, with different activities and a different volume of expenditure reflecting different questions asked and different stages of materials development. This is not to suggest rigid, inflexible advance budgeting, but a general, long-range budget plan that can be elaborated on in terms of detail as emergent needs become clearer.

Any figure or percentage of total budget suggested for evaluation could be supported or challenged, since there is no finite standard to be applied. One might anticipate allocating from 10 to 25 per cent of the annual project budget to evaluation. But the adequacy of even this broad a range depends on whether all evaluative activities are included in the evaluation portion of the budget. For example, the following are evaluative activities but are generally not budgeted as such: project staff visits to experimental classrooms; teachers meeting to discuss their classroom experiences and make recommendations for change; and printing of experimental student materials.

Until very recently, educators were not accustomed to spending substantial sums of money on educational research. Many of the subject matter specialists are still not comfortable with such large-scale spending on research. Some granting agencies have been willing to spend millions on curriculum development but have not accepted a substantial budget item labeled *evaluation*. In some instances they have said that such educational research or evaluation is a more suitable activity for sponsorship by another funding source. Others apparently prefer the pragmatic approach of the so-called action program, where the very existence of the new program or activity constitutes the evaluative evidence the sponsors want and no formal evaluation is launched. Recently the public granting agencies have indicated that they expect systematic evaluation activities as part of the curriculum development programs they fund; but there is as yet no evidence that a strong evaluation budget is an asset to a curriculum proposal.

It is not only the granting agencies that may look askance at high evaluation budgets. Project personnel may also object, not to the activity *per se*, but rather to the fact that evaluation is the largest part of the budget, as it may well be when such items as classroom visiting activities and printing and shipping experimental editions of books for tryout in schools are included under the evaluation label. Thus, what may appear to be a sound budgetary practice may actually wreck the evaluation program.

To obtain a useful evaluation, the way evaluation items are assigned to budget categories is of less importance than ensuring that every needed item appears. This is particularly important in those programs where the shifting of funds to meet an unforeseen contingency or an oversight in budget preparation can be so time consuming as to defeat the purpose of the requested shift. Furthermore, it is critical that all decisions relevant to the evaluation program be made in the light of the requirements of that program. Probably no evaluative activity is without implications for other project activities, and no other project activity is entirely free from evaluative implications. Thus, the important consideration is not so much in what budget category an activity falls, or even who makes what decisions, but rather whether all the needed information is available and taken into consideration before major decisions relevant to evaluation are made.

Evaluation can be run on a shoestring budget, but often the economies are only paper savings, savings that may damage the project if they result in inefficient use of personnel or loss of one-time data collection possibilities. For example, in one $1 million-a-year project, test analyses for one activity were done manually by existing secretarial staff, an inefficient and costly process, because there was no money available for that particular activity. There was no problem in having tests printed; this came from publishing funds. There was no problem of packaging and mailing of tests; this came from the postage and shipping budget. Needed test answer sheets were left over from an earlier activity. But funds for the electrographic pencils necessary if there was to be machine scoring and for computer time were not specifically available and could not be purchased under any other budget category.

A different kind of problem results from the fact that academicians are not used to paying for services and equipment. Many have been without adequate secretarial help, proper equipment, and reasonable services for so long that they feel extravagant in budgeting for items that, in fact, they cannot afford to be without. A research person's time costs a project at least ten dollars per hour, and probably more, and is also scarce. It is extravagant for the evaluator to do his own typing, even if he is a rapid typist, or to be delayed in his work because needed materials have not yet been typed. It is also extravagant for him, or for his secretary, to do routine clerical work.

For projects on college campuses and in school systems, some evaluation items cost less than they would in other situations. If the institution has a computer center, charges are far more modest than is the case where commercial computers must be used. On college campuses consultants are often available at no charge, and some routine services are free or charged nominally. For example, one can often obtain free help on a statistical problem from a colleague, advice that may be sought over lunch or on the way to the parking lot; this is help that would have to be purchased in projects that do not have these professional contacts readily available. (However, university policies may preclude the use of a campus colleague as a paid consultant.) Undergraduate and graduate student personnel are often available on a part-time basis, an arrangement feasible only if they are located at the same physical site; comparable professional services cost more when purchased on the open market.

Farming out parts of the evaluation may sound expensive when an estimate is obtained from an outside research or testing agency, and the cash outlay may support such an impression. However, often this is not the case. First, costs and adequacy of service vary widely among such organizations, and the level of service provided is not necessarily directly related to the cost. It is well to get several estimates and also to check each organization's current reputation for flexibility, quality, and promptness in meeting deadlines and schedules. Second, when on-campus services may mean costly delays, as for example when the campus computers have a three-month backlog, it is probably advisable to go off campus for this service. Third, the cost should be figured not in terms of dollars paid out but rather in terms of real cost of activities. If no money changes hands, if no bills are paid, the activity is still not free. Time expended should be compared with cost of hiring the work out. It may be cheaper to have certain kinds of statistical work done outside by people who do this frequently and are efficient at it than to do it within the study, as a one-time operation, by persons who have no experience with this task, unless a major purpose of the project is to train researchers in such tasks.

One of the new features of budgeting may be the requirement by the funding agency of *cost-benefit ratios*. These constitute an attempt to measure anticipated gain per dollar input and to provide answers to such questions as, "If we put $10,000 more into the evaluation, what extra benefit do we get from it?" While at first glance this seems a reasonable question, the result may be an illogical extension of what Callahan (1962) calls the "cult of efficiency" to still another aspect of education. When an experiment is exploratory—and many project evaluations are and should be—the outcome is uncertain; thus, how can one predict with any degree of accuracy the result of a given increment? Further, the value of an activity may not be in direct relation to the cost, and some activities are essential regardless of cost. For example, classroom visiting is essential; and although it is not possible to predict how useful each visit will be, these visits may make the difference between a successful curriculum and a floundering one. Visits close to home are cheaper than those to distant teachers, but there is no way of predicting whether different feedback will be obtained in more distant places. Yet these are the kinds of price tags the cost-benefit ratio implies. When applied to projects and project evaluations, this technique would seem to reflect the kind of thinking that demands prior guarantee of outcomes before experiments may be launched and that may, in so doing, discourage the most creative experiments.

Particularly for the first year or two of a project, it is helpful to visit other curriculum projects in order to talk about budget items and also to check with their business managers about what supplies are needed for evaluation and what kinds of payments are made in connection with evaluation.[1] This is one way of checking to be sure nothing has been left out of the planning that could reasonably have been anticipated. There will always be unforeseen problems, particu-

---

[1] For lists of science and mathematics projects and their activities, the *Report of the International Clearinghouse on Science and Mathematics Curricular Development* (Lockhart, 1967), issued annually, will provide the needed starting point. For other areas, lists of NSF and OE grants, as well as articles in education journals devoted to a particular subject area, are useful. The ASCD series, "The Changing Curriculum" (ASCD, 1201 16th St. N.W., Washington, D.C. 20036), is helpful, but it may not be current in a particular area or it may not cover that area. See also H. Grobman (forthcoming) for suggestions on such arrangements.

larly the first time any activity or operation is done, and the more potential problems that can be handled in advance, the easier it will be to handle the contingencies.

TIME SCHEDULES

Closely related to budgeting is the scheduling of evaluation activities; this can raise particularly severe problems in large projects. For today's curriculum projects, the traditional leisurely view of research activities is out of the question. Estimates of time and sequencing of project activities, including those involving evaluation, are usually expected by even the most flexible funding sources. Moreover, evaluation activities must conform to, rather than determine, the schedules of the experimental schools as well as those of the rest of the curriculum project. Thus, a clear time schedule, with detailed plans for meeting deadlines, is imperative. Tests must arrive in schools on time to permit administration on schedule. Further, all feedback data must be available to project writers in advance of their rewriting of an experimental edition.

A written breakdown of jobs—what is involved and what the sequences are—is useful for explaining the time requirements to others as well as for helping the evaluator implement his evaluation activities. For example, it is difficult for someone who has not been concerned with testing of large groups to understand why it takes so long to get tests out to the schools and to get test data tabulated. The fact that tests have to be written is not convincing evidence, since this can be done in advance. The printing time for tests can also be an advance operation, though too often it presents a last-minute crisis. But, particularly for projects using a wide geographic area for testing, time for tests to reach the schools and then be mailed back to the project can amount to ten days to two weeks each way. Also, school schedules vary tremendously. Schools open any time from the last week of August to the last week of September; and an end-of-semester test may be administered the first week in January in some schools and early in February in others. All this should be indicated in the evaluation schedule, to help the evaluator plan his activities and also to make the schedule more understandable to his colleagues.

If the time schedule includes process, personnel, services, and materials, it also provides a way for the evaluator to check on whether he has forgotten something critical. For example, if the evaluator has down on paper, where he and others can go over it, each process and product needed to get a test prepared, printed, and mailed to the schools and back, along with dates for each item, he may avoid delay in test mailing. The sources of delay are many. A week or two before the test mailing date, the evaluator may find out that the standard delivery time on special orders of IBM answer sheets is from three to four months after the order is placed. Or on mailing day, the project mail clerk is on his long-scheduled vacation. Or the mailroom reports that it has no heavy-duty mailing envelopes on hand and there are not enough available locally to permit immediate mailing. Or the return address mailing envelopes (being sent with the tests to encourage teachers to return answer sheets promptly) are the wrong size and will not fit into the over-all mailer. While these are managerial problems, unless the evaluator knows what his schedule will be and what supplies and services will be called for and advises the office manager accordingly, the evaluation can hardly run smoothly.

Although the time schedule can be useful in anticipating staff and materials needs and fitting evaluation into the rest of the project, it can also become a Frankenstein's monster. Just as is the case with the listing of project objectives, the evaluator can spend so much time in working out a schedule and refining the time and activities chart that he has no time to do any of the activities he has charted. For some complex educational research projects, the schedules have been computerized, so that the project staff receives computer reports of detailed scheduling and progress relationships. For most of today's curriculum projects, this would provide a plethora of information, interpretation of which would not warrant the time involved in putting the data on the computer and in interpreting the results.

The system used for setting up the calendar and the amount of detail included will vary with the complexity of the project, the experience of the evaluator, and the personal preferences of the evaluator. There are a number of prototypes he can follow, which reflect not only different degrees of detail but also different systems. The most widely known system, *PERT* (Program Evaluation and Review Technique), was developed for management control in business and industry[2] and has been adapted for use in educational research by Desmond Cook (1966) of the Ohio State University Educational Research Management Center.[3] (A sample PERT schedule is presented in Figure 2.)

Insofar as can be anticipated, the over-all evaluation chart or check-

---

[2]See Evarts (1964) for a description of the system and the steps in implementing it.
[3]Cook (1966) includes an annotated bibliography and a list of sources of PERT information. See also Cook (1964) and Stufflebeam (1964).
The Ohio State University School of Education, Education Research Management Center, Columbus, Ohio 43210, maintains current bibliographies on this subject and from time to time has offered short courses on the use of PERT technique in educational research.

list should include a listing of all the kinds of things the evaluator will be doing through the year: how much time, material, and personnel will be required for each activity; the approximate completion dates for each activity; how various activities dovetail with each other and with other project activities; at which points there is flexibility; which activities have a tight schedule and a firm deadline and which ones can be fit in as time permits. In one sense this provides a job description for all the people connected with evaluation; it explains the breakdown of the evaluation budget (or becomes the basis for budget preparation); and it serves to explain who is doing what, when, and why.

BUILDING RAPPORT

It is difficult to think of a curriculum evaluation situation not involving maintenance of rapport by the evaluator with project personnel or with superintendents, supervisors, principals, and teachers who are helping in the testing of experimental materials and who are also potential adopters of the curriculum materials.

RAPPORT WITHIN THE PROJECT

When the evaluator is not an integral part of the project staff, he may be viewed as an outsider who does not understand the project and its concerns and objectives. Even when he is a regular staff member, evaluation may constitute something of a threat to the rest of the project participants. To some extent, the evaluator is a devil's advocate; the good evaluator must ask embarrassing questions. Evaluation does stress strengths, but at some points of curriculum development, the negative—the what-can-we-improve-on aspect—comes to the fore.

Even in a project strongly committed to evaluation, the most tactful evaluator may find himself resented or shunted aside occasionally; as a result, some of his reports may not be given full, thoughtful consideration. This is not a conscious hostility or deliberate disregard of important data; rather, it reflects a very human, very natural unease in the face of criticism, particularly of something dear to one's heart. At times, the ego involvement of some curriculum project people approaches a crusader's zeal. Such ego involvement is an asset to the project and a spur to productivity; but it can make people hypersensitive in the face of evaluative data that indicate less than perfection.

In recent years some highly relevant critiques of experimental materials have been passed off without adequate reflection, with the

FIGURE 2

TABULAR WORK BREAKDOWN FOR ACHIEVEMENT TEST DEVELOPMENT PROJECT

LEVEL 0	LEVEL 1	LEVEL 2	LEVEL 3	LEVEL 4
Achievement Test	Test Booklet	Test Plan	Purpose Objectives Content Specifications	
		Item Pool	Item Writers	
			Test Items	Item Drafts Item Review
		Test Forms	Tryout Forms	Student Directions Administration Directions Tryout Sample Form Assembly Tryout Administration Statistical Analysis Revised Item
			Final Form	Student Directions Administration Directions Norm Sample Final Test Booklet Norm Administration Statistical Analysis Normative Data
	Accessory Material	Manual	Outline Preliminary Draft Final Draft	
		Answer Sheets	Machine-Score Hand-Score	
		Scoring Procedure	Keys Directions	

Source: Desmond L. Cook. *Program Evaluation and Review Technique, Applications to Education*, OE-12024, Cooperative Research Monograph No. 17, Washington, D.C. U.S. Government Printing Office.

Key to diagram:

Circles represent events, that is, the start or completion of an activity.

Solid line represents an activity, that is, a task or job in the project requiring utilization of personnel and resources over a period of time.

Dotted line represents a "dummy activity," one that does not consume time or resources.

The next step in constructing the PERT chart would be to set times for each activity, thereby permitting a scheduling start and finish date and a dovetailing with other project activities.

(FIGURE 2 Cont.)

SUMMARY NETWORK FOR ACHIEVEMENT TEST
DEVELOPMENT PROJECT

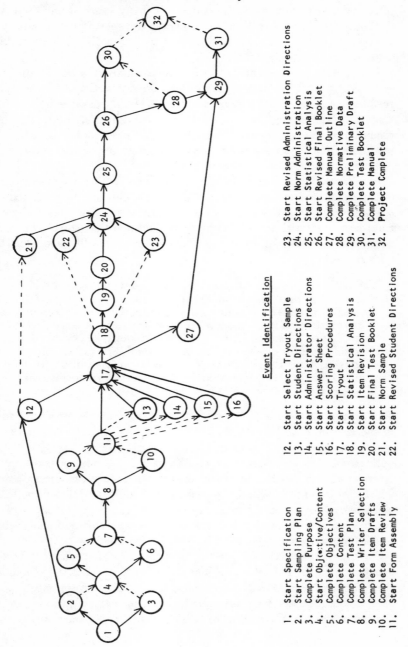

Event Identification

1. Start Specification
2. Start Sampling Plan
3. Complete Purpose
4. Start Objective/Content
5. Complete Objectives
6. Complete Content
7. Complete Test Plan
8. Complete Writer Selection
9. Complete Item Drafts
10. Complete Item Review
11. Start Form Assembly

12. Start Select Tryout Sample
13. Start Student Directions
14. Start Administrator Directions
15. Start Answer Sheet
16. Start Scoring Procedures
17. Start Tryout
18. Start Statistical Analysis
19. Start Item Revision
20. Start Final Test Booklet
21. Start Norm Sample
22. Start Revised Student Directions

23. Start Revised Administration Directions
24. Start Norm Administration
25. Start Statistical Analysis
26. Start Revised Final Booklet
27. Complete Manual Outline
28. Complete Normative Data
29. Complete Preliminary Draft
30. Complete Test Booklet
31. Complete Manual
32. Project Complete

reaction—sometimes verbalized, often not—of: "But he's a psychologist; what else would you expect?"; or "Educators don't understand what we are trying to do"; or "He's a traditionalist and hasn't changed his views of physics (or history or mathematics) for thirty years." Sometimes such criticisms are valid, but this is not always the case. Thus, a natural resistance to direct criticism has tended to reduce the effectiveness of some evaluative activities.

In deciding to go ahead on systematic evaluation, a curriculum project director and his policy committees do not anticipate this type of problem. At one time or another, they probably assure the evaluator that they can accept honest criticism. Nonetheless, there is a good chance that the problem of resistance will arise sooner or later. The evaluator who is forewarned may be able to anticipate some of the difficulties and perhaps minimize them.

Simply the wording of evaluation reports or the cover letters accompanying them can make a difference. The careful balancing of strengths and weaknesses found during the evaluation may reduce the trauma of the critique. A summary of findings that starts out with a statement such as the following may be more readily accepted than a blunter one.

> Since the primary purpose of the reviews was to focus on how materials could be improved, there were more comments on weaknesses than on strengths. However, commentators stressed that in no sense should this be interpreted as indicating dissatisfaction with the materials reviewed or with the ideas on which they were based, but rather that the ideas behind these materials are sufficiently exciting to justify spending considerable further effort in making them even better.

This introduction was followed by two pages citing strengths found in the materials and four pages citing serious weaknesses. Though the recipients were highly sensitive to criticism, they accepted the latter with reasonably good grace. Such an approach is neither coddling nor intellectually dishonest; it is an attempt to create an atmosphere in which the reader is willing to continue reading and listening. Every positive statement made was true. But many reports gloss over the positive to get to what the evaluator considers the real meat of the report, the negative criticism and the faultfinding.

Once a project is sold on the usefulness of a particular kind of evaluative technique, the problem of hostility toward that technique may diminish. For example, in face-to-face confrontation with a group of competent school teachers who have been using a new set of curriculum materials, the writers of these materials may start out sparring,

The following table is taken from a standard form often used for reporting data on student responses to individual test items. An explanation of the table follows; such detailed explanations generally do not accompany the table.

TABLE 5

ITEM ANALYSIS OF FINAL EXAMINATION
BASED ON A SAMPLE OF 740 PUPILS
TESTED IN SPRING 1964

	Per Cent of High and Low Pupils Responding to Each Option*										
Item	A		B		C		D			Total	
Number	High	Low	High	Low	High	Low	High	Low	Key	p	r
1	01	03	13	17	85	79	02	02	C	82	.09
2	34	36	03	09	55	40	08	15	A	35	−.02
3	00	07	01	07	01	05	98	81	D	89	.45
4	03	04	83	59	13	30	01	07	B	71	.29
5	03	01	17	34	10	04	69	61	C	07	.19
6	79	61	19	31	01	05	01	04	A	70	.21
7	13	20	73	49	01	04	14	27	B	61	.25
8	05	08	01	11	04	43	89	35	D	62	.57
9	73	81	07	05	17	05	03	09	B	06	.07
10	01	15	76	44	21	31	02	10	B	60	.34
81	03	11	66	39	05	13	24	37	C	09	−.21
82	81	39	01	16	11	27	07	15	A	60	.44
83	04	26	01	13	03	13	92	44	D	68	.56
84	00	07	71	33	13	31	15	25	B	52	.38

*High group consists of the top 27 per cent of the pupils in the sample on total test score. Low group consists of the bottom 27 per cent of the pupils in the sample on total test score.

Explanation of chart

The first column, *Item Number*, refers to the number of each question on an 84 question, multiple-choice test.

Each question includes four possible alternatives; the double columns labeled A, B, C, and D across the top of the table refer to the answer options for each question. Thus, the columns labeled A refer to those students selecting answer alternative A for a given question.

Under each answer option (A, B, C, D) there are two subcolumns, *High* and *Low*. *High* refers to those students whose total scores on the test were

(TABLE 5 Cont.)

the highest of all students taking the test. And *Low* refers to those students whose total scores on the test were the lowest of all students taking the test. Thus, for item #1, the overwhelming majority of good and poor students (categorized on the basis of over-all success on the test) selected answer *C;* 85% of the high students and 79% of the low students selected answer *C*.

Under the *Total* heading to the far right of the table, the column labeled *Key* indicates the answer considered best by the test writers. Thus, for question #1, answer *C* is correct.

The column labeled *p* indicates the per cent of all students taking the test who selected the correct answer. For question #1, 82% of those taking the test answered correctly. Thus, question #1 was extremely easy for all students.

The last column, *r*, is the biserial correlation (often written as r_{bis}). This is a way of stating mathematically the extent to which a question discriminates between the high-scoring students and the low-scoring students on the total test. Thus, for question #1, an r_{bis} of .09 indicates that this question did not effectively discriminate between these two groups of students. Question #83, with an r_{bis} of .56, was effective in discriminating between good and poor students. Item 81 has a negative r_{bis}. This means that the correct answer was selected more often by the poorer students than by the better students. A majority of the good students selected answer *B*, rather than keyed answer *C*. This is an indication of some kind of trouble either with the item or with the curriculum. The problem may be that the question was incorrectly keyed; that is, that the correct answer is answer *B* rather than answer *C*. Or the question may be stated ambiguously. It may have two correct or equally defensible answers. Or it may be that course materials are misleading.

---

arguing, and testing out the teachers. However, during this preliminary period, if the writers come to respect the teachers as pros, they will be more likely to listen carefully and less likely to waste future time in sparring. In other words, once the informational source stands up to tests for accuracy, intelligence, and usefulness, use of evaluative information from this source is facilitated. There probably will still be a few individuals who cannot cope with this kind of feedback situation; for example, there may be some experts who cannot take criticism from elementary or high school teachers. Insofar as possible, it would be best to exclude such experts from such encounters. Also, with the rotating personnel used by many projects, as replacements are brought in on the writing or the teaching teams, the sparring process may be repeated.

At times, rapport has been jeopardized by the highly technical language used by the evaluator, resulting in his reports being ignored because they are not easily understood or readily usable. For example, a member of the project writing staff, when presented with standard data on individual test items (Table 5), may be told that these can be used to determine strengths and weaknesses of students using the experimental materials. He will probably be given an information sheet explaining what each column represents. But before he can make efficient use of these data, a great deal of time must be spent in figuring them out. The evaluator may feel that any worthwhile curriculum writer should be able to interpret statistical data for himself. The curriculum writer, in turn, is quite likely to feel that any good evaluator should know enough about the curriculum materials to make this interpretation and save the writers the effort. Regardless of who is right, many writers will not take this time, particularly if they have never had training in statistics.

If the evaluator himself presents possible interpretations of data (see illustration below) and then talks these over with the writers, these data may be more functional. (Although the evaluator may overlook some implications of the data, the same danger exists, perhaps to an even greater extent, when the writer, unaccustomed to analyzing such data, makes his own interpretation.) Through this gradual introduction to the interpretation process, the curriculum writer not only may pick up the ability to interpret the data himself but also may acquire the stimulus to do so.[4] The following is an excerpt from a narrative report by a project evaluator, summarizing test data and suggesting interpretations; detailed statistical tables were presented as a supplement to this narrative.

> There is no question that the subject matter is getting across, and that students understand the test items and are able to handle them, as well as the kinds of cognitive skills they involve. Test 3 is easier than the preceding two tests. Perhaps the items themselves are basically easier, or the students may be catching on to the course and to the testing method. (This should be checked against teacher feedback.)
> While many of the items that were relatively easy were memory items (e.g., #1, #3, #8), others go beyond this. For example, #9, #10, #11 involve comprehension and #38 is at the analysis level.

---

[4]Further information on the kinds of uses to which item data on tests can be used is included in Appendix E. See also Wallace (1963) and H. Grobman (1963) for illustrations of the technical reports, which may be necessary to an evaluation and of the interpretive reports which can usefully supplement these.

Note that all items dealing with aspects of energy (#5, #6, #7) are difficult even for the brighter students (i.e., those getting the best total scores on the test). Perhaps the text materials need more work, or the teachers may not have spent enough time on the unit.

On item #23, poorer students (those in the lowest third in terms of total test score) did not get this at all. They consistently chose incorrect answer b. The question is not ambiguous, as most of the other students found it relatively easy. Thus, if the area this item tested is an important one, perhaps the teachers should be alerted insofar as the slower students are concerned.

According to the student grades assigned by teachers (these are indicated on many of the answer sheets), teachers have not taken seriously the project's statement that this test is more difficult than the usual teacher-made test, and a score of 60% correct is about average (C). Some teachers are considering 60% as D— and others, as failing. It is likely that this will produce adverse reactions to the course among students and their parents.

RAPPORT WITH EXPERIMENTAL SCHOOLS

With the idea of curriculum experimentation approaching the dimensions of a fad, some teachers have been faced with highly experimental and radically different materials for at least one of their classes or subject areas each year, with no reduced teaching load to compensate for the additional planning time involved in teaching new and often more demanding courses. The incentive to perfect the presentation of one new curriculum may be decreased because of the real possibility that it, too, will be changed before long. Negative reactions toward experimental curricula may grow even more severe unless school systems become more selective in trying out innovations.

Unfortunately the resistance to a curriculum experiment may come not in outright refusal to cooperate but in agreement to cooperate and then failure to meet commitments. Some curriculum projects have urged that experimental schools lighten the classroom load of the teacher who uses the experimental classroom materials and prepares feedback reports for the project. Others have been able to pay the teacher a small sum to compensate him for time spent in writing reports and attending project meetings. Such morale-building arrangements for participating teachers should be considered.

Teachers may also be concerned about pupil time required for various types of tests in the evaluation. It may seem that the pupil has little time left to learn the materials on which he is being tested. For example, if the project being evaluated is a one-month unit in English, there may be a general ability test at the start to describe the pupils included in the experiment, and there may be pre- and post-experiment achievement and attitude tests of one or more kinds. Thus, easily one-quarter of the classroom time for the unit may be taken up with project testing, in addition to the time the teacher himself may want for quizzing and testing. Even in a one-semester or year-long course, where there is a multiplicity of objectives to be tested with written test instruments, and pre- and post-experiment data as well as periodic testing is desired, there may be strong teacher resistance, or the teacher may participate in the experiment and then fail to give all the requisite tests. The pupils, too, may resent frequent tests and become less cooperative.

A different problem in maintaining rapport concerns fear of data leakage or embarrassment resulting from the manner in which the findings are released: that some teachers will be labeled as better than others; that some school systems will be labeled good and others less good; that visitors from the project will make value judgments concerning the adequacy of the teaching and classroom management, which will be passed along to supervisors and other administrative personnel. Such considerations as these may be completely peripheral to the intent of the evaluation, yet they may preclude a valid evaluation.

Some novice evaluators assume that entry into the schools and development of rapport will present fewer problems when the curriculum is a local or regional one and the evaluator is a member of the participating school system staff. This is often not the case. Many teachers and principals will resist having an insider collecting information that may be potentially damaging to them. This is not a question of distrusting the individual investigator, but rather of suspecting the pressures that may be put on him and the later uses of file data after this investigator goes on to a different assignment.

Relevant to this concern about possible damaging uses of evaluative data is the need for making and honoring, in substance as well as in form, the absolute guarantee that information collected will never be released in such a way as to embarrass those assisting the project. Whether or not such violation of confidence is intentional, it is damaging.

In releasing statements on the evaluation, care must be taken to present data and conclusions in such a way that they cannot be identified with individuals, schools, or school systems. The researcher would be well advised to modify such references as "a Michigan community with 1960 official population of 14,273," or "the only major city in New Jersey with a single public high school, a red brick building in the center of town," or "the only senior high school in the state with a woman principal." In many instances the generalizability of the evaluation results will not be adversely affected by replacing such specific descriptions with the more general statement of "a city of between 10,000 and 20,000 population," or "a three-year urban senior high of between 1,500 and 2,000 enrollment." And in those cases where reporting is adversely affected, it is suggested that the evaluator respect and learn to live with this limitation. If previous researchers had not honored their commitments to keep data confidential, he would probably not now have entree. If he does not honor his present commitments, not only will the reputation and acceptability of his project's materials suffer, but the next researcher probably will be refused entree to the school system.

The role played by teachers trying out project materials can do more than make or break the evaluation activities; it can also enhance or jeopardize the acceptability of the curriculum produced by the project. Projects that indicate, as many have, that they represent cooperative efforts of subject matter specialists and educators must prove this by their actions. This is not only a matter of involving classroom teachers as peers in the writing of the materials but also of listening to them on other occasions. When feedback is sent in and not considered, the teachers will be alienated. Despite instructions to the contrary, teachers will often ask questions in the course of feedback reports or include a series of questions in a mailing of student answer sheets; this may indicate a failure to read instructions, or it may be the teacher's way of testing whether the project pays attention to teacher reports.

Some studies have alienated teachers, either during teacher preparation institutes or at the start of the school year, by asking the teachers to take tests intended for students in the new curriculum. Granted, it may be useful for evaluative purposes to know whether teachers have mastered these materials; but it is nonetheless insulting to the teachers to give them a test intended for their students. Even if there were not other limitations inherent in this practice,[5] it should be entirely abandoned if for no other reason than the fact that it impedes the building of morale.

---

[5]If the test is intended for students, probably teacher scores will be relatively high, with little leeway for gain. Furthermore, a gain of two points, from an initial score of forty-five correct out of fifty questions to a retest score of forty-seven correct, may mean something far different than a two-point gain from twenty-five to twenty-seven correct out of fifty questions.

MAKING TEACHER PARTICIPATION EASIER

Teachers participating in project evaluations may not come through with requested data because of the inconvenience involved. The teacher's lack of a postage stamp can mean that feedback reports are not mailed in or are mailed only after some delay. (Items not mailed promptly are more likely to be mislaid.) The teacher may not know how much postage to put on an envelope for the return of answer sheets, and the school may not have a postal scale. While a prompt trip to the post office is feasible, it is highly unlikely. Materials to be sent back by teachers will be mailed more promptly if the teacher is provided with return address, stamped envelopes large enough to hold the expected mailing.[6]

Some projects have found it desirable to ask for the return of all test booklets (booklets including test questions) for project tests. The cost of such return mailing is minimal and can save later problems; for example, despite instructions to destroy test booklets after one-time use, many teachers will save such experimental instruments, and the project may be haunted afterwards with these preliminary tests and even with the results of outside research studies using these tests, years after the experimental editions on which they are based are obsolete.

Where commercially published standardized tests are provided to the teacher, it would be a goodwill gesture to suggest that these be retained and to advise where additional answer sheets may be purchased, should the school wish to re-use such test booklets at a future date. Test scoring keys (giving correct answers) and the publisher's teaching manual should also be provided for such tests, so that, should the school wish to score and record the test results before answer sheets are returned to the study, it may do so readily. (While some projects have been able to furnish schools with individual student scores on the standardized tests used during the curriculum evaluation, this is an expensive and cumbersome task, and several projects that have promised such data have later regretted the commitment.)

Teachers are often asked to write reports based on their reaction to classroom use of the materials. While this appears to be a simple assignment, it can become tedious to the teacher who has 200 or more different students each day or who teaches a single elementary class of thirty-five students with no assistance and no secretarial help. To minimize the effort required in preparing reports, some studies

---

[6]For suggestions on test mailing procedures and other procedural details in evaluation, see H. Grobman (forthcoming).

have provided the teacher with an extra copy of the curriculum materials and have suggested that notes be written directly in the book, either in the margin or on the blank left-hand page. It is far easier for the teacher to do this than to explain, in a separate report, the page and line he is commenting on. One project perforated the pages of the teacher's copy of its materials for easy removal; others have provided the teacher with a looseleaf copy of materials to facilitate prompt preparation and mailing back of reports at the end of a section or unit. Here, too, return address, stamped envelopes are a convenience and may result in a higher return of reports.

On occasion, face-to-face feedback is easier for the teacher to provide, even though it is more expensive for the project. An hour's talk over coffee with a visitor from the project may seem easier to the teacher than fifteen minutes of writing. A teacher would often prefer going to a meeting or conferring at project headquarters, time consuming though these may be, to writing a lengthy report. Particularly where relatively short distances are involved, oral feedback may be a more reliable way of getting needed information, provided the atmosphere of the feedback situation is conducive to frank reactions.

The teacher's convenience in terms of his personal time schedule should also be considered. College people seem to think that vacations, Thanksgiving weekend, and Christmas and Easter vacations are ideal times for meetings and extra report writing. School teachers rarely agree. For non-vacation periods, December is an unusually busy time and is unsuitable for extra commitments and demands. The first week or two of school in September and the last week of each semester are trying for teachers. In many schools enrollment and scheduling do not become stable until the second or third week of school, and so testing immediately upon the opening of school is not optimal if students are to be followed through the year. Not all end-of-experiment tests need to be scheduled the last week of school. For subject matter tests, this may be indicated, but if the student is to be tested on changes in such general aspects as problem solving ability or attitude toward the subject resulting from a year-long course, changes that have not occurred by early May are unlikely to occur between then and the end of the school year, and in early May there is less pressure for testing time. Further, insofar as it is practical, teachers should have some leeway in timing. Thus, tests should not be scheduled for November 16 or April 10, but rather for the week of November 16 or the week of April 10, or still better, for some time during a two-week period.

6

What are Reasonable Expectations

In a laboratory the scientist finding a statistically significant difference between control and experimental groups is reasonably confident that a valid difference exists. He does not ask, "In experimental frogs, is a change in heartbeat of ten beats per minute enough?" or "Could this difference reflect experimental error, the one chance in 100 or 1,000 where the difference occurs through chance?" Rather, he is concerned with whether a difference is statistically significant and with his degree of confidence in rejecting the null hypothesis, and he equates statistical significance with practical significance. Yet the same scientist, in looking at the results of a test of student achievement, may say quite categorically, "There is only a four-point difference between control and experimental groups. This implies that I have been wasting my time." This four-point change may represent one standard deviation; it may be statistically significant beyond the .001 level. Yet the scientist may use quite different criteria in looking at a report of elementary or high school achievement test results than he uses in reading a research report in *Science*. If the scientist, who is accustomed to dealing with statistics and tests of significance, has difficulty in appraising the relative implications of educational statistics, the problems encountered with experts in literature, linguistics, industrial arts, and history may be even more acute.

Perhaps one reason the subject matter specialists hold unrealistic expectations concerning the magnitude of change in students using project materials is the ego involvement of such specialists in the project work. Some have become completely absorbed in this work, sometimes with a messianic fervor; they often expect to revolutionize the student's knowledge, attitudes, and skills, not only in the subject area under treatment but also in terms of a carry-over of these mental processes to other subject areas. They expect a wholly new and discrete universe to open up for their students, and this change is expected to be so complete that there will be virtually no overlap either with that student's previous test behavior and skills or with those of students taking parallel existing courses.

In the subject areas traditionally offered—English, biology, social studies—certainly there must be some overlap between the new and the old curricula, even when the new is quite radical. It is generally agreed that the new biology, chemistry, foreign language, and mathematics materials break new ground and include different emphases; yet there is still overlap with traditional courses in coverage, as well as in method of handling the materials. Also, not all previous teaching was bad, and not all teaching of new project materials is exemplary. With new materials, the chances of a teacher implementing the inquiry aspects of the subject are perhaps enhanced, but this is not guaranteed; and, though such implementation may have been more difficult and less frequent with earlier, traditional materials, it certainly was not precluded.

In the case of subject areas not formerly taught, students can have different degrees of prior familiarity. Before the development of new math, it is unlikely that students had any familiarity with set theory; thus, one can expect these learnings to be exclusive to new math students. However, although anthropology, economics, or sociology may not have been either included as discrete units or integrated into social studies materials, there are a great many ways in which children pick up relevant ideas from nonschool sources. Television programs near election times give information about sampling techniques, population shifts, and regional characteristics. Visits to museums, traveling, and simply receptive contacts with adults and peers result in more experiences and cognitive and affective responses than we usually give students credit for.

Unless an economics test deals with trivia (size of the national income in 1963, the first year the U.S. average family income before taxes exceeded $3,000, the year Keynes died), the student who has never had a course in economics will be able to answer some questions; and if he is bright, he will probably answer more items than some duller students who have had economics. In one study of economics test scores, some tenth-grade students with no economics outscored some twelfth graders who had studied economics. Students who had not studied economics between tenth and twelfth grades nonetheless gained six to seven points in test scores in the two-year period.[1] This evidence does not necessarily mean that something is wrong with the test or with the test statistics, but rather that general intelligence influences test scores and that maturation and the environment pro-

[1] Unpublished study by H. Grobman on *Test of economic understanding*, using scores of 10,000 students and several hundred teachers tested by school systems.

vide a great many stimuli, and, in most academic areas, that learning through course materials is only one facet of the student's cognitive and affective intake.

The more our testing focuses on the higher cognitive skills of analysis, synthesis, and evaluation, rather than on knowledge and direct application of this knowledge, the less plausible it will be to produce valid tests that separate, with little overlapping of scores, those students who have been exposed to one particular curriculum and those who have not. When testing is limited to definitions of terms used in areas of chemistry not covered in traditional courses or of terms that have a specialized meaning in economics, a meaning different from that in common usage, perhaps only students who have studied the specialized curriculum will be able to respond correctly. However, no single subject area or course is the exclusive domain for teaching critical thinking skills. While one curriculum may foster such skills more effectively than another, the skills will not be exclusive to students in that curriculum, and tests that measure these skills will doubtless have an overlap of scores for students of different curricula. The problem of obtaining measurable change unique to one curriculum is even greater in the area of values and attitudes. Many educators forget how difficult it is to bring about change in attitudes and in behavior, and subject matter specialists may never have thought about this at all. Further, even if such change occurs, given the difficulties of accurate measurement of attitudes, it may not be reflected by student scores on the instruments used.

Unless the curriculum project sets realistic sights in terms of what change is anticipated, there is likely to be disillusionment and recrimination later. As Bloom (1964) points out, the preschool years of life are those in which the environment is most influential in setting patterns and developing abilities. These patterns become less and less susceptible to change; change during adolescence is far more difficult to bring about and, the evidence appears to indicate, is generally less dramatic than is the case in earlier years.

A single junior high school course in social studies may aspire to change the student's views of himself in relation to others in American society and in the world. But the seventh-grade teacher sees the child only after he has had thirteen years of living and six or seven years of previous schooling, all of which may have taught him, perhaps indirectly, the exact opposite of what the new curriculum is trying to put across. In fact, one part of the seventh-grade social studies course, or other courses the same year, may contradict what another part is emphasizing.

One high school science teacher expressed deep concern over the fact that some of her very best students were failing or getting D's in English, when they were accustomed to A's. Further discussion indicated that she had encouraged a questioning attitude, saying that nothing should be accepted simply because it is stated dogmatically or authoritatively; rather, one should ask the reasons why. Her science students were then asking "Why?" in English class, and the English teacher did not approve of this questioning of his authority. Through a trial-and-error process, the students in this situation learned that the norms in science called for inquiry and that those in English called for acceptance without questioning. Yet, such a learning was defeating the very purpose of the science course, that is, to develop an inquiring attitude toward all phenomena.

Even if there is consistency of approach within the grade level, regardless of how well the curriculum is developed, societal influences often limit rather than enhance the chances of successful implementation of project aims. Can one really hope to teach urban children that lawfulness is the best way to achieve desired ends, if the most dramatic positive results they have seen come only when lawlessness is threatened or erupts? Can the desirability of peaceful approaches to problems be taught effectively when so many of our popular heroes are warriors, and when, in the United States, we have traditionally elected winning generals as President? How effectively can the new economics units, in use in many elementary schools in New York, teach the importance of working hard and saving money to buy the things one wants, when the State of New York is embarking on a get-rich-quick advertising campaign to increase sales of tickets for the state lottery, which provides funds for improving public education? How effectively can one teach the value of education and its importance in modern life, an aim of most curricula, given the widely circulated reports of semi-literate popular entertainers amassing millions or of athletes whose annual salary equals a Nobel Laureate's total income for a decade?

No curriculum operates in a vacuum. This does not mean that curriculum materials are not important or that they cannot make some difference. However, one course, for one year, will not revolutionize the intellect of most students. What, then, is a realistic expectation? Is it worth improving the curriculum? If so, how much change in students must occur before the change can be considered successful? When is a statistically significant difference also an educationally significant difference?

Given the student's limited contact with the new curriculum—at best, generally less than an hour a day for 180 days—and the slow rate at which people change, particularly in such basic skills as how they think and how they solve problems, one must expect only modest measurable changes to occur in students during a single year. During the first year the teacher is using the new curriculum, these changes may be even smaller than will be the case in later years, after the teacher has become accustomed to the new content and method and is able to work out his pacing of the materials more effectively. One cannot expect student performance drastically to reflect a new thrust in emphasis of one curriculum until this is mirrored in other curricula at the same grade level and at other grade levels, as well as in the prestige symbols, the college entrance examinations, the scholarship awards, and other honors related to the academic system.

Each project must determine its own criteria for success. If one of the project's criteria concerns developing a new way of thinking on the part of the students, then it must decide the extent to which it hopes to change students and what proportion of students it hopes to change. It is unrealistic to expect all students exposed to the curriculum to change in the desired direction. What proportion of students does the project realistically hope to affect? If the project is concerned with widespread diffusion of an idea or of new content, then the measure of success is the extent of diffusion over a period of time, with the time period sufficiently long to reflect the delays caused by the textbook adoption regulations of many states.

A school system planning textbook adoptions may use different criteria in evaluating project materials than does the project itself. The school system may weigh the expenditure of six dollars per child on learning-to-read materials against the advantages of spending less on books and more on teachers, while the project may be concerned only with whether children using these materials learn to read more rapidly.

As the project initiates its plans and continues its work, the continual refinement of its expectations and the growing recognition of the realities of the situation should make possible a relatively clear delineation of its criteria for success. The project evaluation should focus on these. Others outside the project will have different criteria and may check out the project's work in terms of these. The project should be cognizant of such other criteria and should consider the extent to which it should provide information relevant to these criteria. Schools considering use of materials may have one set of questions to ask. Funding agencies have other questions. For projects supported by public funds, there is an implicit obligation to report to that public in terms of its concerns. Even though no project is likely to complete these reporting jobs, it certainly can have more useful information available than has generally been the case to date. This, then, is the project's evaluation function.

APPENDIX A

IDENTIFICATION OF ABBREVIATIONS

AAAS	American Association for the Advancement of Science
ASCD	Association for Supervision and Curriculum Development
BSCS	Biological Sciences Curriculum Study
CASEA	Center for Advanced Study of Educational Administration, University of Oregon
CBA	Chemical Bond Approach
CEEB	College Entrance Examination Board
CHEM STUDY	Chemical Education Materials Study
ERIC	Educational Research Information Center
IME	Interaction of Matter and Energy
JCEE	Joint Council on Economic Education
NDEA	National Defense Education Act
NLSMA	National Longitudinal Study of Mathematical Abilities
NSF	National Science Foundation
OE	United States Office of Education
PSSC	Physical Sciences Study Committee (later changed to ESI—Educational Services Incorporated, and then to EDC—Educational Development Center, Incorporated)
SMSG	School Mathematics Study Group
UICSM	University of Illinois Committee on School Mathematics

APPENDIX B

SUMMARY OF CATEGORIES OF THE
TAXONOMY OF EDUCATIONAL OBJECTIVES

In considering the categories of the *Taxonomy*, it is important to keep in mind that, by definition, the system is a taxonomy; that is, it is hierarchical, and so, for each ascending category, all lower categories must be included. Thus, a cognitive task cannot be categorized as *analysis*, level 4 of the hierarchy, unless it includes *knowledge* (level 1), *comprehension* (level 2), and *application* (level 3).

Knowledge

1. *Knowledge* involves the recall of specifics and universals, the recall of methods and processes, or the recall of a pattern, structure, or setting. The recall situation involves little more than bringing to mind the appropriate material, although some alteration of the material may be required.[1]

1.1 *Knowledge of specifics*—the recall of specific and isolatable bits of information, including *knowledge of terminology* and *knowledge of specific facts.*

1.2 *Knowledge of ways of dealing with specifics*—the ways of organizing, studying, judging, and criticizing, including methods of inquiry, chronological sequences, standards of judgment, and patterns of organization through which the areas of fields are determined and internally organized. This includes: *knowledge of conventions*, of ways of treating ideas and phenomena (e.g., correct form and usage in writing); *knowledge of trends and sequences* (e.g., continuity in American history of certain trends); *knowledge of classifications and categories* or the arrangements or divisions fundamental to a given subject; *knowledge of criteria*, that is, the criteria by which judgments are made; *knowledge of methodology*, the methods of inquiry in a subject (e.g., the way of testing a hypothesis).

1.3 *Knowledge of universals and abstractions in a field*, the major patterns by which phenomena and ideas are organized, including *knowledge of principles and generalizations* and *knowledge of theories and structures*, such as the principles and generalizations that present a systematic view of a field, problem, or complex phenomenon (e.g., the seven organizing themes of biology, including genetic continuity, interrelation of structure and function, etc.; the major divisions into which physics is organized).

While the above categories range from the highly specific to the abstract, the tasks covered by these categories nonetheless involve only recall of knowledge.

Source: Adapted from Benjamin S. Bloom (Ed.) *Taxonomy of educational objectives, the classification of educational goals, Handbook I: the cognitive domain.* New York: McKay, 1956. Adapted with permission of the publisher.

[1]The *Taxonomy* itself provides specific illustrations of test questions for each category and subcategory of the system.

Intellectual Abilities and Skills

Abilities and skills refer to modes of operation requiring more than knowledge and emphasize mental processes of organizing and reorganizing materials, either given or remembered, to achieve a specified purpose.

2.   *Comprehension* means that the individual knows what is being communicated and can make use of the idea without necessarily seeing its fullest implications. This includes what is commonly termed "direct application."

2.1 *Translation*—a paraphrasing or rephrasing from one language or form of communication to another, as from graph to prose, chart to graph, or prose material to formula or other symbolic statement (including art, cartoon, music, poetry).

2.2 *Interpretation*—a reordering or rearrangement of material.

2.3 *Extrapolation*—an extension of trends or tendencies, prediction, consequences, corollaries.

3.   *Application* involves the use of abstractions in particular and concrete situations; it includes what is commonly termed "indirect application" and involves tasks not directly replicating those done earlier.

4.   *Analysis* requires the breakdown of a communication into constituent elements so that the relative hierarchy of ideas and/or interrelationships is made explicit.

4.1 *Analysis of elements*—identification of the elements included in a communication (e.g., ability to distinguish fact from hypothesis).

4.2 *Analysis of relationships*—recognition of the connections and interactions among parts (e.g., consistency of hypotheses with given assumptions or information).

4.3 *Analysis of organizational principles*—recognition of the organization or structure, both explicit and implicit, in a unit (e.g., inferring an author's philosophy or biases from his writings).

5.   *Synthesis* requires the putting together of elements and parts to form a whole, the rearranging or recombining of units into a new, unique (for that individual) product.

5.1 *Production of a unique communication* does not include all new writing or plans, but requires a systematic, excellent organization of ideas and statements or an effective presentation.

5.2 *Production of a plan or proposed set of operations* that satisfy the requirements or specifications of the task, as, for example, the development of a new way for testing a hypothesis, the design of a new instrument, a unique plan for solving a mathematics problem.

5.3 *Derivation of a set of abstract relations* may be a new way of classifying things or an explanation of phenomenon or the derivation of new (for that individual) propositions.

6.   *Evaluation* involves making systematic qualitative or quantitative judgments based on criteria developed by the individual or given him.

6.1 *Judgments in terms of internal evidence*, using internal criteria such as logical accuracy, consistency, absence of internal flaws, etc.

6.2 *Judgments in terms of external criteria* requires systematic judgment with selected or remembered criteria, as, for example, comparison with other materials, general standards of excellence, consistency with an arbitrary or nonarbitrary standard.

APPENDIX C

QUESTIONS RELEVANT TO CHANGE

The following are indicative of evaluative questions of concern to school systems in considering new curricula. Provision by projects of relevant information will facilitate such consideration. Many of the questions are relevant to project studies of the change process.

DECISION MAKING

How do we arrive at decisions? Who should be involved?

NEW PUBLICS

Have we plans to communicate with parents of students who do not participate as well as with parents of students who do participate? Have we developed strategies for diffusion of results in a personalized way to all who should have this information?

PHASES

Do we know where we are on the continuum: in planning, developing a climate for change, initiating an experiment, trying out pilot materials, diffusing and stimulating a new program? Have we plans for continuing improvement so that we do not become static?

POLICY AND ADMINISTRATIVE ARRANGEMENT

Does school board action include adequate provision for reeducation of personnel and extra costs accompanying the change process? Have administrative arrangements been made to support change; for example, changed role expectations of persons in leadership capacities? Has the superintendent made adequate provision for curriculum counsel from a number of sources to provide for proper evaluation of ideas and programs? Have the resources of the state department of education been thoroughly utilized?

IN-SERVICE

Is the development of effective in-service programs for teachers contingent on finding sufficient time at appropriate intervals for intensive programs? Will this lead to consideration of newer methods of school organization that offer possibilities for redeployment of staff time? Will the in-service program lead to a longer school day or year? Are our library and other professional materials available and adequate for teachers and administrators to study?

Source: Excerpted from Robert R. Leeper (Ed.) Appendix: Study questions. *Assessing and using curriculum content*, Washington, D. C.: Association for Supervision and Curriculum Development, 1965. p. 17–25. Copyright © 1965 by the Association for Supervision and Curriculum Development. Used by permission of the editor and publisher.

Is extensive and external consultant help for various phases of the in-service program to be made available; for example, in the study of children's learning problems and the specific problems related to the teaching of different content areas? Have provisions been made for teachers and other staff members to observe the pròject in operation in situations similar to their own? How must the role of the teacher be redefined to make possible adequate in-service education? Will the development of leadership among teachers be fostered and encouraged? What role should state departments of education play in the development of in-service programs?

PRESERVICE

How effective is communication between schools and teacher preparation institutions and between projects and teacher preparation institutions? How can communication be improved? Are colleges and universities ensuring that new teachers are well informed about curriculum innovations and sensitive to the instructional processes appropriate to their implementation? Are teacher preparation institutions providing in-service opportunities for their own staff members both in and outside the field of education? Do professors have a general understanding of the goals and methods of all projects in the appropriate fields? Are schools and teacher preparation institutions cooperating to provide for continuity in the education of teachers?

Study Questions Related to Assessing
New Projects and Their Effect on Learners

TYPES OF LEARNERS

Are the materials clearly designed for a particular group—for fast, average, slow learners? For a particular age level? Do project materials vary sufficiently to benefit learners who have different cognitive styles (e.g., inquirers and noninquirers, those who work well with symbols and those who work well with concrete objects)? Are the materials more appropriate for boys or for girls?

EFFECTS ON LEARNERS

What effect might the new program have on the anxiety levels of learners? What opportunities do learners have to strengthen their intellectual independence? To what extent are learners encouraged to be creative? Are such behaviors restricted by the project materials or services? As a result of the new program, are the pupils likely to become more excited about learning than they have been previously? Are learners encouraged to develop facility with a variety of materials and approaches to learning? What attitudes and values might learners acquire through the project? What kinds of behaviors —cognitive, affective, psychomotor—are learners encouraged to exhibit?

STABILITY OF STUDENT GROUPS

How will student turnover affect the success of the project? What special arrangements must be made for students who transfer into the school? What prerequisites are required if they are to participate in the new project?

Study Questions Related to Assessing
New Projects and Their Effect on Teachers

DEMANDS ON TEACHERS

What new content must the teacher master? What new teaching strategies are required? Are these clearly specified? What programs of teacher preparation will be necessary?

TEACHER CHARACTERISTICS

Are there specific teaching skills demanded; for example, working with large groups, small groups, individuals, audiovisual aids? Is experience an important factor to be considered? Is openness to new ideas essential for teachers in the project? Is teacher personality a significant factor? Must teachers have a great deal of free out-of-class time?

Study Questions Related to Assessing
Curriculum Project Resources

GOALS

Do project goals differ from our goals? If so, in what way or ways? Should our goals be modified? Is the conflict too great for us to consider this project? Do the goals of a given project differ from goals of other similar projects? Should the differences affect our choice? Do the goals imply specific instructional methods? How willing and able are staff members to use these methods?

DEVELOPMENT OF MATERIALS

What are the backgrounds of those responsible for developing project materials? Were the materials field tested? In what kinds of schools? Are available data and descriptions of the test situation(s)—for example, students, teachers, communities—sufficiently complete to allow us to make an informed decision? What other data do we need? Are potential problems and ways of handling them described in the project materials? Can we handle the problems? What theory of learning is assumed in the materials? Is it one we can accept? How was grade-level placement of subject matter determined?

EVALUATION OF MATERIALS

What criteria were used to evaluate materials as they were developed and tested? Was information about project materials obtained from test-school teachers during the development of the project? If so, how was this information used to modify the materials? As materials become obsolete, is there any effort to provide revisions?

CHARACTERISTICS OF MATERIALS

What kinds of materials are available with this project—for students, for teachers, for parents, and for other community members? What types of activities are implied by the materials? Are activities dependent upon materials specifically designed for the project—films, records, special laboratory equipment? Are the materials designed as a unified program with little opportunity to alter sequence or type of use? Must we adopt or may we adapt? Do the materials require teachers and learners to act in ways consistent with the methodology of the discipline represented by the project? Do materials emphasize both content and process? Is the relation between the two clear? Are materials based upon needs of learners as well as on the structure of the discipline? Are materials from the project consumable? What is the cost of initial materials? Of replacements? Does the project or a publisher supply materials or must the school design and produce them? Are there tests available that are consistent with new materials? To what extent can they be used as teaching tools? Are the materials sufficiently flexible to be used in a highly individualized way?

ASSISTANCE FROM PROJECTS

Does the project provide opportunities to see the project in action? Are there films, demonstration centers? Is consultant help available to assist in the implementation and evaluation of the project? Is such assistance critical? What kind of continuing information is available from the project? What kinds of resources does the project provide to assist in the introduction of the project in the community, to help parents understand the project?

ORGANIZATIONAL CHANGES

Are we aware of the resources needed to make the project successful: kinds of talent, amount of time, additional funds, committees, in-service programs? How can we utilize the talents of our own teachers? Will we require outside help? What in-service courses, institutes, workshops will be necessary to help our teachers prepare to work on the project? How can we provide time for experienced teachers to participate in in-service work? For new teachers? Is a particular school organization (self-contained, nongraded) necessary to implement the project successfully? Are we willing to make the necessary changes? Is the project more beneficial when used with a group of a particular size? Can we establish the necessary groups? What is the time required of the teacher for planning and implementing the project? Would regional curriculum centers to disseminate information about projects be useful? Can we assist in establishing such centors?

RELATION OF PROJECT TO PRESENT PROGRAM

Does the project require totally new courses, or does it fit into our present structure? What new time commitments are required in subject areas? In what ways would the new project affect levels where it is not in use? In what ways would the new project affect other areas; for example, a science project that assumes student familiarity with a particular kind of mathematics? What adjustments may be needed so that balance can be maintained in the total instructional program? Is the project developed in sequence? Does this sequence parallel our own?

Study Questions Related to Assessment

ADEQUACY OF DATA

Do we have initial data on learners—their achievement, their motivation, their personalities? Do we have initial data on teachers—their strategies, their motivation, their knowledge, their personalities? Do we have these data at many stages during the implementation of the project? Would a model assist us in making a continuing assessment? For example:[1]

T1 (initial appraisal)	*During a Project*	*T2 (final appraisal)*
Set up instruments to assess	Observers analyze the strategies of students, teachers	Set up instruments to assess
students' { achievement, personality, motivation		students' { achievement, personality, motivation
	Assessors analyze materials and their effect on teachers and learners	
teachers' { satisfaction, strategies, knowledge		teachers' { satisfaction, strategies, knowledge

What happens to learners as people and to learners as learners as a result of the project? What happens to teachers as people and to teachers as teachers? Do changes justify the time and funds expended?

REASONS FOR CHANGE

Are we contemplating a curricular change because we are committed to excellence in education and because we realize that society is changing and that education therefore must change? Is change in this system a result of a continual planned evaluation of our program? Is there general dissatisfaction with the existing program among teachers, administrators, and other members of the community? Are we considering change only or largely because of changes in other school systems or because new funds will become available? Would a change stimulate each staff member to study and improve his performance? Are we being pressured to change by selfish interests of a segment of our system?

SCHOOL AND COMMUNITY FACTORS

Does the community understand the role of the school well enough to support a change if the need for change is indicated? Does the board of education support warranted innovations? Are administrators prepared to give constructive leadership to bring about change? Do we have a sufficient number of teachers who are willing to work toward major changes? Do we

---

[1]Developed by Ira J. Gordon during group deliberations at the Conference on which this publication is based.

have access to outside sources to assist us with a change; for example, university or college personnel, state department staff members, project representatives? Does our school system have a healthy climate in which the insecurities of the change process can be tolerated?

EXTERNAL FACTORS

Does the state department prescribe tests, curricula, textbooks, and instructional materials? Do universities exert influence on our program development? Do accreditation agencies exert influence on our program development?

Study Questions Related to Future Action

STAFF MEMBERS

Are we clearer about our goals than before we instituted the change? Are we involving more of the appropriate persons in major decisions? Are we more open to new and different ideas? Has resistance to change increased? Decreased? Has the general professional climate changed? How? Have more avenues of communication opened? Closed? Are staff members deriving more professional satisfaction from their work? Have new leaders been identified as a result of the change? Are staff members in general more effective? Less effective?

PROGRAM

Have we identified significant omissions in our goals? Have we identified strengths or weaknesses of which we were not aware before? Have we developed new and more effective ways of working with individual learners? Are we better able to provide for individual learners in all areas? Is balance in the program greater or less? Are we able to utilize teachers' and learners' strengths to the advantage of each individual?

APPENDIX D

SOME EVALUATION QUESTIONS CONCERNING
A CURRICULUM IN BIOLOGY

BSCS Versions

To what extent has the BSCS accomplished its goals in these materials? Are these goals appropriate? Are these same goals appropriate for further revisions of BSCS biology? What psychology of learning is implemented?

What is the total impact of the BSCS program? What effect (empirical evidence as well as informed judgement) has BSCS had on other biology teaching; that is, on teaching, books, tests, etc.? To what extent are the BSCS courses actually implemented in the schools? What BSCS materials are used and what other materials are used to supplement these? How are BSCS materials adopted in schools? Are some means of adoption more effective than others?

Is the writing team approach effective as a way of preparing curricular materials? What size writing teams are best for what jobs?

What is the effect of BSCS Versions on other new courses in later grades in high school and college, and on student performance on these?

What is the most effective sequencing of materials within a version? Where are students experiencing difficulty? Why? Are certain teaching behaviors more effective in stimulating the desired learnings? What is the contribution of a well-used BSCS laboratory? Are the lab exercises developing inquiry skills? Reasoning skills? General skills? Other noncontent abilities?

What skills do students retain in later years and is it easier to relearn some skills that have been forgotten? Do these "savings" differ from those of other biology students? Do BSCS students do better in college? In what kind of college? In what way?

What evaluation tools must be developed to determine the impact of BSCS biology on the student? Can these be used as predictive instruments, e.g., for college success in certain science experiences, for operation in the adult community as a citizen? What are the facets of "good" evaluation tools? How can BSCS tests be evaluated? What long-term evaluation seems desirable to check achievement of stated aims and goals of biology teaching?

Laboratory Blocks

Are the Blocks consistent with their stated aims? Are more skills, understandings developed? Does Block use change teacher and/or student attitude toward biology, science, etc.? Do Blocks develop something unique? What are identifiable traits reflecting Block use two or three years after completion by student (or by teacher)? What are student savings (in learning) from Block use? Do Block and non-Block students differ in the BSCS Second Course? In college?

Source: Adapted from Hulda Grobman. Needed research in high school biology. *The American biology teacher.* XXVII, No. 9, Nov. 1965, 705–7. Used with permission of the publisher.

How do teachers select particular Blocks? Are there teacher personality factors concerned with adoption and continued use of a Block? Why have some teachers dropped use of the Blocks?

At what part of the year is use of a Block most effective? How can Blocks be more effectively integrated with version work? How do Blocks work to supplement non-BSCS courses? Is six weeks the optimal time for the Block?

Teacher Preparation Program

What happens in the various kinds of teacher preparation programs for BSCS Biology?

Are the BSCS monographs on teacher preparation (BSCS Special Publication Series) being used?

Are the programs recommended by the BSCS producing effective BSCS teachers? Are such programs changing teacher knowledge, attitudes, and practices? Can the in-service teacher change, and if so, how can change be brought about most effectively? Are NSF Summer Institutes (and/or In-service Institutes) effective in preparing teachers for BSCS biology?

Is collegiate teacher training consistent with development of BSCS objectives and with practice of successful BSCS teachers? What effect has BSCS biology had on the preparation of teachers?

Can we identify effective teachers of BSCS biology and the factors related to this effectiveness? How can this effectiveness be developed in others?

Has the BSCS improved biology teaching? Has the BSCS changed teacher attitudes and methods of teaching? What is the teacher interpretation of the BSCS concepts and of the problem-solving process?

What is the teacher interpretation of what he is doing in the BSCS classroom? What is the place of teacher-held objectives in implementation of BSCS biology?

How effective is the BSCS Area Consultant program in teacher orientation?

Have the BSCS materials helped teachers who are not using BSCS student materials with their classes?

External Exams

What effect does CEEB (College Board) have on biology teaching, on teacher and student attitudes and subject matter? Does it change teacher (and/or administration) perception of what must be done in biology classrooms? To what use are CEEB Biology Test scores put by college placement offices, others? Is the CEEB test "fair" in terms of use of test results?

Are there standardized tests—other than the BSCS tests—that reflect the aims and objectives of BSCS? What is the effect of use of other biology and general science tests on teaching of BSCS biology?

To what extent do the test instructions or the behavior of the test administrator bias the results of testing?

General

Can we measure "inquiry" ability? How is this related to other BSCS tests? To other biology tests (e.g., College Board)? To later activities—college, citizenship, science career success?

What is the role of laboratory experiences in science education? What are measurable skills and intellectual advantages in the laboratory approach? Can the inquiry abilities gained through lab work be identified? What reasoning skills can be developed as the result of the laboratory experience? How can the way a laboratory experience is presented affect the expected outcomes of the laboratory?

Does background of undergraduate NSF research fellowship holders reflect a specific kind of high school biology background?

APPENDIX E

SOME USES OF TEST DATA IN FORMATIVE EVALUATION

George P. Hollenbeck
The Psychological Corporation
New York, New York

Test results can be very useful to the curriculum developers. Several such ways will be illustrated below. These are only examples of many variations.

The usual test analyses provide several types of data. One type is the total test score, providing the mean score, the standard deviation, perhaps percentiles for a group, and the range of scores. Another is item data, an index of item difficulty, the per cent of students responding to each of the alternative answers to a given question, and perhaps an item discrimination index. Another type relates test score or item score to such other variables as grade level, type of school, or curriculum used. Each of these types of data can be viewed from different viewpoints. The professional tester, interested in improving the test, may see the test as too easy, the spread of scores as too small, a particular item option as drawing too many or too few responses. The same scores, viewed by the curriculum developer, may indicate that the students are understanding the curriculum content and that most students are achieving the objectives, although some are not clearly distinguishing between the concepts in two particular items. The curriculum evaluator must be able to wear both of these hats. He must be able to caution that perhaps the test is too easy, but report that the students are achieving what the curriculum developer intended.

Some data collected early in a junior high school project on general industrial processes will be used for examples. A pilot study of a three-day segment of the curriculum was conducted. At the end of the unit, students took a 25-item multiple-choice test, with each question having five answer options. Although several types of evaluation data were collected, only some data from two schools, both of them potential users of the curriculum, will be examined here.

The mean test score of the total group was 11.9 correct. For School A the mean was 15.6 and the range was 11 to 21; and for School B the mean was 8.2 and the range was 2 to 15. Fifty per cent of School A scores exceeded the highest School B score.

While the data presented above are only "test data," the curriculum developer has at hand much useful information. Since the curriculum contents and the instruction at both schools were very similar, and differences exist in student ability between the two schools, hc is rather quickly led to consider the appropriateness of his curriculum. Perhaps the entire curriculum unit is much too difficult for School B students; if the curriculum is designed for use in both types of schools, two levels of curriculum may be necessary. An alternative hypothesis is that the fault is not with the entire curriculum

---

Adapted from George P. Hollenbeck. Using the results of evaluation. Paper prepared for a symposium on "The role of evaluation in national curriculum projects," at American Educational Research Association meeting, New York, February, 1967. Used with permission of the author.

unit but only with part of it. The next step is an item-by-item examination of success in each part of the curriculum. Such an analysis would reveal whether the difference between schools exists throughout the curriculum segment or only in certain parts. Test items can be examined individually, by subject groupings and by skills required.

Such item data from School A will be examined, although A-B comparisons might suggest interesting hypotheses. For School A, the average item difficulty was .62 (i.e., 62% of the students answering correctly), quite acceptable from the viewpoint of individual measurement. This may also be quite acceptable from the curriculum developer's viewpoint, but he should examine the items carefully and attempt to judge the extent to which mastery of each item is desired.

To provide more information for the analysis, the group was divided into upper and lower halves on the basis of total test score, and the per cent in each of these groups responding to each option of each test item was determined. These data are presented below, for three of the test items.

SCHOOL A ITEM ANALYSIS DATA
FOR CURRICULUM REVISION

Item number	Correct answer	Group	Percent Selecting Each Answer				
			A	B	C	D	E
1	#C	Upper half	0	0	100%	0	0
		Lower half	0	0	86%	0	14%
14	#E	Upper half	0	0	0	0	100%
		Lower half	0	29%	7%	21%	43%
24	#E	Upper half	79%	0	7%	0	14%
		Lower half	29%	7%	43%	7%	0

These data illustrate the differences which may appear in one short, 25-item test. The first item is an example of a *mastery item*. Nearly every student got the correct answer. The content of the item was quite general, and students would be expected to answer correctly. Since the few missing the question marked option E, the curriculum developer might examine option E for clues as to why it was attractive.

Item 14 presents a different picture. First, data indicate that the lower-half students are not getting the item, while the upper-half students are. The question then is "What went wrong?" The wrong responses were concentrated in options B and D. The item was:

14. In quality control, parts are inspected and tested for
    A. quantity.
    B. superior quality.
    C. strength and hardness.
    D. exactness in shape.
    E. falling within acceptable limits.

Most students (and all of the high group) chose option E, the correct answer. One of the key ideas in the curriculum was that mass production is dependent upon the fact that parts are *not* manufactured to exact standards of size and quality. Rather they fall within acceptable limits. But 29% of the lower group chose option B and 21% chose D where "superior" and "exactness" are the attractors. The data indicate that a substantial segment of the low group still had the everyday idea of quality control. At this point, the curriculum developer must go to work to remedy the lack of understanding.

Item 24 presents still different problems. Note that the correct answer is option E, not option A as would be expected from a glance at the response data. Few students answered correctly. The high group and the low group select different answers, but neither group is selecting the correct answer. By the same type of analysis as presented for item 14, the curriculum expert can take this information, examine the content of the question and each alternative, hypothesize about what went wrong in the curriculum, and then check to see whether his hypothesis is valid.

While the analysis thus far has been from the view of the curriculum developer, questions should also be considered from a testing standpoint, to insure that it is the students, or the curriculum and not the test questions, that are at fault.

There are other uses of test information in the formative evaluation of a project. Test questions can be divided into subgroups on the basis of subject classifications and/or ability classification. Particular questions or item responses may be examined in relation to other questions or response alternatives.

Using test data in the ways described does not complete the evaluation job. To be most valuable these data must be used in conjunction with the other evaluation data collected, such as experiences of the teachers and pupils; but if the test data and the other available information can be brought together at an early stage of curriculum development, the test information can be an important aid in revising the curriculum.

BIBLIOGRAPHY

American Educational Research Association. Information storage, retrieval and dissemination. *Educational Researcher*, Supplement 1967.

American Educational Research Association. *AERA monograph series on curriculum evaluation*. Chicago: Rand McNally, 1967-————.

Anderson, Richard C. The comparative field experiment: an illustration from high school biology. *Proceedings, ETS invitational conference on testing, 1968*. Princeton, N.J.: Educational Testing Service, forthcoming, 1969.

Association of American Geographers—National Council for Geographic Education. Final report of the NDEA Geography Institutes evaluation program, 1965 summer institutes. Washington, D.C.: The Association, November, 1965.

Atkin, J. Myron. Some evaluation problems in a course content improvement project. *Journal of Research in Science Teaching*, I, No. 2, 1963, 129–32.

Atkin, J. Myron. Behavioral objectives in curriculum design. *Science teacher*, 35, No. 5, May 1968, 27–30.

Backstrom, Charles H. and Hursh, Gerald D. *Survey research*. Evanston, Ill.: Northwestern University Press, 1963.

Bagley, William C. Editor's introduction. In Bode, Boyd, *Modern educational theories*. New York: Macmillan, 1927.

Bennis, Warren G. *Changing organizations*. New York: McGraw-Hill, 1966.

Bloom, Benjamin S. *Stability and change in human characteristics*. New York: John Wiley & Sons, Inc., 1964.

Bloom, Benjamin S. (Ed.) *Taxonomy of educational objectives, the classification of educational goals. Handbook I, the cognitive domain*. New York: McKay Company, 1956.

Bode, Boyd H. *Modern educational theories*. New York: Macmillan, 1927.

Bond, Guy L. and Dykstra, Robert. The cooperative research program in first-grade reading instruction. *Reading Research Quarterly*. II, No. 4, Summer 1967.

Boyd, Robert D. and DeVault, M. Vere. The observation and recording of behavior, Chapter IV, *Review of Educational Research*, XXXVI, No. 5, December 1966, 529–51.

Brickell, Henry M. *Organizing New York State for educational change*. Albany, New York. State Department of Education, 1961.

BSCS Newsletter. Boulder, Colorado, BSCS, P.O. Box 930, Boulder, Colorado.

Buros, Oscar K. *Reading tests and reviews*. Mental Measurements Yearbook Monograph Series. Highland Park, New Jersey: Gryphon Press, 1968.

Buros, Oscar K. *Science tests and reviews* (working title). Mental Measurement Yearbook Monograph Series. In preparation.

Buros, Oscar K. (Ed.) *The sixth mental measurements yearbook*. Highland Park, New Jersey: Gryphon Press, 1965.

Buros, Oscar K. (Ed.) *Tests in print*. Highland Park, New Jersey: Gryphon Press, 1961.

Cahen, Leonard S. An interim report on the national longitudinal study of mathematical abilities, *The Mathematics Teacher*, LVIII, October 1965, 522–26.

Callahan, Raymond E. *Education and the cult of efficiency*. Chicago: University of Chicago Press, 1962.

Campbell, Donald R. and Stanley, Julian. Experimental and quasi-experimental designs for research on teaching. In Gage, N. L. (Ed.), *Handbook of research on teaching*, Chapter 5. Chicago: Rand McNally, 1963. (Also reprinted in pamphlet form, Rand McNally, 1966).

Carlson, Richard. *Adoption of educational innovations*. Eugene, Oregon: Center for Advanced Study of Educational Administration, University of Oregon, 1965.

Carlson, Richard O. *et al*. *Change processes in the public schools*. Eugene, Oregon: Center for Advanced Study of Educational Administration, University of Oregon, 1965.

Cook, Desmond L. A new approach to the planning and management of educational research. The PERT Project, School of Education, The Ohio State University, October 27, 1964 (mimeographed).

Cook, Desmond L. *Program evaluation and review technique, applications to education*. U.S. Department of Health, Education and Welfare, Office of Education, OE-12024, Cooperative Research Monograph No. 17. Washington, D.C.: U.S. Government Printing Office, 1966.

College Entrance Examination Board. The curricular appropriateness of the science achievement tests. Princeton, N.J.: College Entrance Examination Board. January 1967 (Printed letter to interested institutions and individuals).

Cronbach, Lee J. Course improvement through evaluation. *Teachers College Record*, 64, No. 8, May 1963, 672–83.

Easley, J. A., Jr. Curriculum development, teacher education and educational research. Paper read at Allerton House to the University of Illinois College of Education Faculty, Urbana, Illinois, January 6, 1967.

Easley, J. A., Jr. Evaluation problems of the UICSM curriculum project—a case study. Urbana, Illinois: UICSM, undated (mimeographed).

Easley, J. A., Jr., Kendzior, Elizabeth, and Wallace, Robert. A 'bio-assay' of biology tests. *The American Biology Teacher*. XXIX, No. 5, May 1967, 382–89.

Ennis, Robert H., and Millman, Jason. *Cornell critical thinking test*. Form X. Ithica, New York: Robert Ennis, Cornell University, 1961 (unpublished).

Evarts, Harry F. *Introduction to PERT*. Boston: Allyn Bacon, 1964.

French, John W., and Michael, William B. (Co-chairmen) *Standards for educational and psychological tests and manuals*. Prepared by a joint committee of the American Psychological Association, American Educational Research Association, and National Council on Measurement in Education. Washington, D.C.: American Psychological Association, Inc., 1200 Seventeenth St., N.W., 1966.

Galbraith, John Kenneth. *The affluent society*, Boston: Houghton Mifflin, 1958.

Glaser, Robert *et al*. Studies of the use of programmed instruction in the classroom. Technical Report 1, University of Pittsburgh Learning R and D Center. Cooperative Research Program OE 2-10-057 and OE 4-10-158. Pittsburgh, Penna.: Learning R and D Center, University of Pittsburgh, May 1966.

Gordon, Ira J. Assessing theories of instruction. Paper prepared for the ASCD Commission on Instructional Theory. Gainesville, Florida: University of Florida, School of Education, June 2, 1966 (mimeographed).

Grobman, Arnold B. *Toward better curricula: the role of the Biological Sciences Curriculum Study*. New York: Doubleday, in press.

Grobman, Hulda. Some comments on the evaluation program findings and their implications. *BSCS Newsletter*, 19. (BSCS, Box 930, Boulder, Colorado), September 1963, 25–29.

Grobman, Hulda. Classroom testing and the biology teacher: an annotated bibliography. *The American Biology Teacher*, XXIX, No. 4, April 1967, 282–85.

Grobman, Hulda. Needed research in high school biology. *The American Biology Teacher*. XXVII, No. 9, November 1965, 705–7.

Grobman, Hulda. *Decisions and processes of developmental curriculum projects*. Chicago: Rand McNally, forthcoming.

Harris, Chester W. (Ed.) *Encyclopedia of educational research*. A project of the American Educational Research Association. New York: Macmillan, 1960.

Hills, R. Jean. *A second analysis of communication and status: the dynamics of a research center*. Occasional papers. Eugene, Oregon: Center for the Advanced Study of Educational Administration, University of Oregon, 1966.

Hollenbeck, George P. Using the results of evaluation. Paper read at the annual meeting of The American Educational Research Association, New York, February 1967.

Hurd, Paul DeH. *Biological education in American secondary schools, 1890–1960*, No. 1, BSCS bulletin series. Boulder, Colorado: Biological Sciences Curriculum Study, 1962.

Klinckmann, Evelyn. The BSCS grid for test analysis. *BSCS Newsletter*, 19. (BSCS, Box 930, Boulder, Colorado), September 1963, 17–21.

Krathwohl, David R., Bloom, Benjamin S., and Masia, Bertram B. *Taxonomy of educational objectives, the classification of educational goals*. Handbook II: affective domain, New York: McKay, 1964.

Krathwohl, David. Statement at a seminar on inquiry, New York University, winter, 1967.

Kropp, Russell P., and Stoker, Howard W. The construction and validation of tests of the cognitive processes as described in the taxonomy of educational objectives. Cooperative Research Project No. 2117. Washington, D.C.: U.S. Office of Education, February 1966.

Kurtz, Edwin B., Jr. Biology in *Science—a process approach. The American Biology Teacher*, XXIX, No. 3, March 1967. 194–5.

Lake, Dale G., and Miles, Matthew. *The assessment of social functioning*. New York: Teachers College Press, forthcoming.

Leeper, Robert R. (Ed.) *Assessing and using curriculum content*. Washington, D.C.: Association for Supervision and Curriculum Development, 1965.

Lockart, J. David. *Report of the International Clearinghouse on Science and Mathematics Curricular Developments, 1967*. A joint project of the American Association for the Advancement of Science and the Science Teaching Center, University of Maryland. College Park, Maryland: University of Maryland, 1967.

Lutz, Frank, and Iannocone, Lawrence. *Understanding educational organizations.*, in press.

McCoy, Eleanor. Untitled manuscript on UICSM history. Urbana, Illinois: Curriculum Laboratory, University of Illinois, in preparation.

McGuire, Christine H. An evaluation model for professional education.

Proceedings, ETS invitational conference on testing problems, 1967.
Princeton, N.J.: Educational Testing Service, 1968.

Mager, Robert F. *Preparing instructional objectives.* Palo Alto, Calif.:
Fearon Press, 1962.

Medley, Donald M., and Mitzel, Harold E. Measuring classroom behavior by
systematic observation. In Gage, N. E. (Ed.), *Handbook of research on
teaching,* Chapter 6. Chicago: Rand McNally, 1963.

Neihoff, Arthur H. (Ed.) *A Casebook of social change.* Chicago: Aldine,
1966.

Oppenheimer, A. N. *Questionnaire design and attitude measurement.* New
York: Basic Books, 1966.

Pikaart, Len (University of Georgia), and Hand, Edith F. (West Georgia
College). Evaluation of a large-scale in-service mathematics institute.
Paper read at the annual meeting of the National Council on Measure-
ment in Education, February, New York, 1967.

The Psychological Corporation. A study of the relationship of selected school
and teacher characteristics to student performance on the BSCS comprehensive final examination, 1961–62. New York: The Psychological Corporation, 1963 (mimeographed).

The Psychological Corporation. *A report of the first-year evaluation of the
Developmental Economic Education Program (DEEP).* January 1968.

Riley, Matilda White. *Sociological research, a case study.* New York: Harcourt, Brace & World, 1963.

Rogers, Everett M. *Diffusion of innovations.* New York: Free Press, 1962.

Rummel, J. Francis. *An introduction to research procedures in education.*
Second ed. New York: Harper & Row, 1964.

Science. Privacy and behavioral research. *Science,* 155:535–6, February 3,
1967.

Scriven, Michael. The methodology of evaluation. In Tyler, Ralph W.,
Gagne, Robert M., and Scriven, Michael. *Perspectives of curriculum evaluation,* American Educational Research Association monograph series on
curriculum evaluation, No. 1. Chicago: Rand McNally, 1967.

Selltiz, Claire; Jahoda, Marie; Deutsch, Morton; and Cook, Stuart W. *Research methods in social relations.* Revised ed. New York: Holt, Rinehart
& Winston, 1966.

Shaw, Marvin Evert, and Wright, Jack Mason. *Scales for measurement of
attitudes.* New York: McGraw Hill, 1967.

Smith, Alfred G. *Communication and status: the dynamics of a research
center.* Eugene, Oregon: Center for the Advanced Study of Educational
Administration, University of Oregon, 1966.

Stake, Robert E. An emerging theory of evaluation—borrowings from many
methodologies. Paper read at The American Educational Research Association meeting, New York, February 1967.

Stake, Robert E. Testing in the evaluation of curriculum development,
Chapter IX, *Review of Educational Research,* XXXVIII, No. 1, Feb. 1968.

Stanley, Julian. (Ed.) *Improving experimental design and statistical analysis.*
Seventh annual Phi Delta Kappa symposium on educational research.
Chicago: Rand McNally, 1967.

Stauffer, Russell G. (Ed.) *The first grade reading studies: findings of individual investigations.* (Reprinted from *The Reading Teacher.*) Newark,
Delaware: International Reading Association, 1967.

Stufflebeam, Daniel L. *An application of PERT to test development.* Columbus, Ohio: Evaluation Center, School of Education, The Ohio State University. February, 1964 (mimeographed).

Thompson, John M. (Ed.) Teachers, history, and NDEA institutes, 1965. Report of a survey team. Sponsored by the American Council of Learned Societies under a contract with the United States Office of Education. New York: American Council of Learned Societies, 345 East 46th St. and Washington, D.C.: the American Historical Association, 400 A Street, S.E., 1966.

Tyler, Ralph W. New dimensions in curriculum development. *Phi Delta Kappan,* September 1966.

Walbesser, Henry H. Curriculum evaluation by means of behavioral objectives, *Journal of Research in Science Teaching,* I, No. 4, 1963, 296–301.

Wallace, Wimburn L. The BSCS 1961–62 evaluation program—a statistical report. *BSCS Newsletter,* 19. (BSCS, P.O. Box 930, Boulder, Colorado), September 1963, 22–24.

Watson, Goodwin, and Glaser, Edward M. *Watson-Glaser critical thinking appraisal.* New York: Harcourt, Brace & World, 1964.

Webb, Eugene J., Campbell, Donald T., Schwartz, Richard D., and Sechrest, Lee. *Unobtrusive measures: nonreactive research in the social studies.* Chicago: Rand McNally, 1966.

Welch, Wayne W. *Science process inventory.* Cambridge, Mass.: Wayne Welch, Harvard Project Physics, Harvard University, 1966.

Wilder, R. L. The role of intuition. *Science.* 156, May 5, 1967, 606–10.

Wooton, William. *SMSG: the making of a curriculum.* New Haven: Yale University Press, 1965.

Yeager, John L., and Lindvall, C. M. Evaluating an instructional innovation through the observation of pupil activities. Paper read at The American Educational Research Association meeting, New York, February 1967.

INDEX OF AUTHORS

INDEX OF SUBJECTS